THE BOOSTER

How Ed Martin,
The Fab Five
and the Ballers from the 'hood
Exposed the Hypocrisy of
a Billion-Dollar Industry

THE BOOSTER

How Ed Martin,
The Fab Five
and the Ballers from the 'hood
Exposed the Hypocrisy of
a Billion-Dollar Industry

CARL MARTIN
WITH JIM MCFARLIN

First published in the United States
by M4O Books

M4O Books is a unit of Men For Others LLC
23247 Pinewood St.
Warren, MI 48091
info@thebooster.net
TheBooster.net

For information about this book, contact the publisher
at the above address or (email, website addresses)

Information about special bulk quantity sales to qualified institutions
and organizations are available from the publisher at the above addresses

Copyright 2018 by M4O Books
All rights reserved

ISBN 978-0-692-07616-3
Library of Congress Control Number: 2018936998

Cover, dust jacket, photo section, and text design by Jacinta Calcut
Image Graphics & Design
image-gd.com

Photograph of author on dust jacket courtesy of Solin Vance

Printed in the United States of America
by Edwards Brothers Malloy
Ann Arbor, Michigan

Without limiting the rights under copyright reserved above, no part of this book may be reproduced, scanned, stored into a retrieval system, transmitted, or distributed in any printed or electronic form or rendered, reproduced, or excerpted in film, video, audio or visual form without written permission in advance. Please do not participate in or encourage piracy of copyrighted materials in violation of the publisher's rights.

*Life is a reciprocal exchange.
To move forward,
you have to give back.*

       Oprah Winfrey

CONTENTS

Preface | ix

1 Boxing Out | 1

2 Hustle Play | 14

3 Training Days | 28

4 Pickup Games | 40

5 Running Up the Numbers | 53

6 The Hook | 67

7 The Assistant Coach | 80

8 Getting into the Game | 91

9 Give and Go | 103

10 Inside the Fab Five | 128

11 Piling up Assists | 142

12 Crunching the Numbers | 154

13 The Raid: Full Court Press | 167

14 Choosing Sides | 191

15 Taking it to the Hole | 213

16 Final Stat Line | 238

    Afterword | 243

    Acknowledgments | 245

PREFACE

It's almost unbelievable how the course of your entire life can change in a simple, everyday moment.

For my father, Ed Martin, it was just a knock at the front door.

It came early in the evening of Friday, February 16, 1996. On the other side of his door was a mountain of a man, a young man Ed knew well. It was Robert "Tractor" Traylor, the 6-foot-8, 300-pound star power forward for the University of Michigan basketball team.

Now, some people might be surprised to see a nationally known, Division I, Big Ten hoops hero standing on their porch, but Ed Martin barely blinked and the two exchanged smiles. Traylor was from Detroit, where we lived, and Ed had helped support him and his family financially since high school. To Robert and many other Detroit PSL (Public School League) ballers, Ed was a benefactor. An angel. A mentor.

Some of those players continued receiving his money after they entered college, so for many people that made Ed Martin a booster. But he certainly wasn't a conventional one, and as a man he was ever so much more than that.

On that momentous Friday night, Traylor and four of his U-M teammates waited in the shiny '95 Ford Explorer idling at the curb. Along with Traylor was teammate Maurice "Mo" Taylor, the 1995 Big Ten Freshman of the Year and also a longtime recipient of Big Ed's largesse. With them were teammates Louis Bullock, Willie Mitchell, and Ron Oliver. With Taylor at the wheel, they were headed to a party in the city to convince a hotshot high school recruit from Flint to join them on the court in Ann Arbor the coming fall.

The recruit wedged into the SUV among the U-M players was Mateen Cleaves, the steel-hard guard with the dazzling smile. He was making an official recruiting visit to Michigan.

In need of some cash to party hearty, the group knew where to turn. They didn't need an ATM because they knew they always had an AEM: Ask Ed for Money. In fact, I'll wager that Taylor and Co. sent Robert Traylor to the door rather than go *en masse* because "Tractor" and his family had long been among Ed's personal favorites.

Ed handed over some bills – the exact amount is lost to history – and the "party bus" was on its way.

However, in the wee hours of Saturday, February 17, fate took a different turn. At about 5 a.m., on their way back to Ann Arbor, Taylor lost control of the Explorer and the vehicle rolled over.

Only by the grace of God was no one critically injured.

The only serious injury was sustained by Traylor, who fractured his right arm and was lost for the season. But that was far from the only damage that occurred. Due to the notoriety of the occupants involved, a one-car crash on an icy Michigan freeway became coast-to-coast headline news by the following morning. The press wanted to know what the players were doing in Detroit until at least 4:30 a.m. Why were they taking a young recruit more than thirty miles beyond campus in violation of NCAA rules? And the more glaring question: how could a college sophomore on scholarship afford to cruise around in a gleaming, $30,000, top-of-the-line Ford Explorer Limited Edition?

Those are good questions. They deserve better answers. They demand more full and complete explanations than they have received up until now in countless column inches of articles and seemingly endless hours of air time. This is the only book that will tell the full story.

My name is Carl Martin. I am Ed Martin's son.

The Wolverines had a home basketball game against Indiana that afternoon and I planned to attend. But on the other end of the phone line was my father. He asked if I had heard what happened, about the overnight accident.

There was concern in his voice for the players. But for himself, there was neither panic nor dismay. Neither of us had to say the words, but we both knew the role that my father had in the events leading up to the rollover. And more. Because Ed Martin had played an active part in the lives of Mo Taylor, Robert Traylor, and other players at Michigan, he soon would be part of any investigation.

We knew that from that day forward, things were going to be different. Just how different, we could never have foreseen.

Carl Martin
April 2018

CHAPTER ONE

Boxing Out

The thing I remember most about that February morning in 2003 – in fact, the only vivid memory I still have of that day after all these years – is sitting in the front row of the church, the row reserved for the immediate family, just staring straight ahead at the casket.

There was bright sun and freezing cold outside in Detroit that day, and inside Greater New Mt. Moriah Missionary Baptist Church there was a constant hum behind me of movement and emotion. People tell me there were white orchids and pink carnations that seemed to cover the entire expanse of the pulpit. But I couldn't hear or see anything else. Nothing else mattered.

I could not stop looking at that box that held my father, Ed Martin. Eddie Lewis Martin. Fast Eddie. Uncle Ed. Big Money Ed. What name you knew him by depended on which of his many social and business circles you knew him from.

He was an electrician for Ford Motor Company more than thirty years, long since retired. He was "the numbers man," head of a sprawling illegal gambling empire on the streets of Detroit, using Ford plants as his base of operations. He was a man about town who enjoyed being the life of the party, seeing and being seen wherever the Big Event was happening, always dressed to the hilt. He was a benefactor, a kind of Robin Hood of the 'hood, an admirer of talent who gave away hundreds of thousands of dollars to people in need – especially financially strapped young basketball players and their families in the 1980s and '90s. Eventually that became, shall we say, problematic.

He was father and fanatic, hustler and husband. Anyone who knew my father only through his involvement as the key figure in the University of Michigan men's basketball investigation of the 1990s may have some other names for him. There were strong opinions about Super Booster Ed Martin, the man at the epicenter of the fall of the Fab Five, which some have labeled one of the biggest sports scandals of the 20th century. As for me, I knew him as Dad. He was my mentor, my role model, my supporter, my friend. Did I love him? I spent 15 months in prison to protect him and his secrets.

He shouldn't be laid out in that casket. Not now. Not yet.

That's not to say I thought he was Superman. Like the old folks say, we all got to go sometime. But just days before, I was talking to him in his room at Henry Ford Hospital and he seemed fine. He was sedated, maybe a little pissed off about having to be in the hospital, but fine.

For weeks he had been suffering with a pain in his leg and hadn't given it much thought. However, when the pain became excruciating, my Aunt Lillian drove him to Henry Ford on West Grand Boulevard. He was quickly admitted. The diagnosis was a blood clot in his leg. It was being treated with medication.

When I saw him in the hospital, Dad was his usual chatty, charismatic self. "Carl," he said, "when I get out of here, remind me I've got to see so-and-so. Son, make sure you go check on your mother."

There was no way I left his room that night saying to myself, "Damn, he won't be with us very much longer." No, I walked to my car confident not only would Ed Martin be around for a long time to come, but he probably would be checking out in the next day or so.

He was just 69. He had his energy, his gift of gab – he was cool.

That's why the phone call that came early the morning of February 14 hit me like a Thomas Hearns jab to the mouth. Because it was so unexpected, because of how my life changed from that moment on, that phone call is still the dominant memory of my life to this point. It is the event I can't shake.

It wasn't even Henry Ford Hospital that called. My mother, Hilda, phoned my house about 1 a.m. "Carl, the hospital just called me," she trembled. "They said we have to come right away."

I remember thinking, "Oh, shit! He's dead? The hospital doesn't call you for any other reason that time of night. Well, let me get up and go on over there."

As I drove to the hospital, I think I was in shock. I kept saying to myself, "For real? For real? So this is how it ends, huh? How jacked up is it that you lead a whole life giving to people, raising a family, taking care of your business and all that, and in the end so many people just let you down? What is the lesson in that?"

At Henry Ford we got the word: pulmonary embolism. The blood clot broke free from his leg, traveled up to his lung and killed him. Just like that.

I knew he had been depressed for quite a while. The previous May, after a relentless four-year federal investigation, Dad agreed to plead guilty to conspiracy to launder money in connection with the University of Michigan basketball scandal. For some time, he had been twisting in the wind, awaiting the date of his court appearance.

My cousin, Detroit-based writer Marsha Lynn Philpot, was the last person in our family to see Ed alive. In her opinion he looked more bedraggled than she had ever seen him before. "He had grown a beard, and it was a sort of scraggly, unkempt, Marvin Gaye-ish kind of beard, which was totally uncharacteristic of him," she said. He was usually clean-shaven, but when he did have a beard, a Fu Manchu or whatever, it was immaculate. That was a real signal that he was under a lot of stress.

"He had experienced years of very grueling investigation by the government," Marsha Lynn said, "and he was in a state of perpetual scrutiny. He was like an animal that had been cornered, and he balked at that feeling because he was a very garrulous and free-spirited person."

On top of that, his wife, my mother, was battling lung cancer that had metastasized to her liver and other organs, and Dad worried about her constantly. The fact that so much of his wealth was gone by this time and he couldn't care for her the way he wanted to made him all the more depressed. And when federal prosecutors initially went after her, too, despite her faltering health, it crushed him.

"He was particularly undone by the involvement of the Feds with his wife," Marsha Lynn said. "That, probably more than anything else, deeply bludgeoned him, the fact that they would involve her in this."

But my father was one of the strongest dudes I've ever known. He would not have wanted to check out under any of these difficult circumstances. He would have wanted to stay around and face the future head on.

My personal sense of disbelief was one thing. Additionally, Ed's death sent shock waves across many corners and communities in Detroit and beyond. His obituary merited sixteen paragraphs in the sports section of *The New York Times*. I'll bet the agents from the FBI, ATF, IRS and the rest of the governmental alphabet soup that spent millions of dollars and employed a virtual army of attorneys and accountants to bring my dad down must have felt a sense of justice interruptus. They got Big Ed Martin to plead guilty, but his death meant he never served time.

However, in possibly the most vivid example of how engaging and magnetic my dad could be, his attorney, Bill Mitchell, said he was contacted by some of the FBI agents who prosecuted him, asking if he thought it would be appropriate for them to attend the funeral. The same people who wanted to send him to prison now wanted to pay their respects to him.

Mitchell could never remember ever receiving such a request in more than thirty-five years as a criminal defense lawyer. He told the agents that for a variety of reasons, he thought it wasn't the best idea for them to be surrounded by Ed's friends and relatives. After hearing that reasoning, they agreed.

Then there were all the Detroit-reared hoop stars, some who made huge money in the NBA. These were men he had supported in countless ways over the years and they could breathe a sigh of relief over not having to repay their debts. These were big-name ballers like Jalen Rose, Maurice Taylor, Louis Bullock and Chris Webber.

Ah, yes, Chris Webber. Is there a luckier brother on the face of the earth? Webber has led a charmed life ever since he rejected the Detroit Public School League to play his high school ball in the cushy suburbs at Detroit Country Day School. After three state championships, he was recruited to the University of Michigan where he became the marquee-player of the Fab Five, the most famous freshman recruiting class in college basketball history.

It was Webber who overcame calling the notorious "no time-out" that effectively cost U-M any chance of winning the 1993 NCAA Division 1 basketball championship against the University of North Carolina. He left Michigan early for the pros, becoming the No. 1 overall draft pick, NBA Rookie of the Year, and a five-time NBA All-Star.

In a preliminary discussion with the prosecuting attorney, Ed stated he gave Webber $280,000 in cash and gifts over the years. Webber testified to a grand jury that he either couldn't recall or didn't think he received such proceeds. Who could forget such a thing? Who would lie about it in a federal court? If he wasn't paying the rent on his off-campus apartment in Ann Arbor, who did he think was? The hoops fairy?

Webber was indicted for perjury, but before his trial could begin, Dad died. And without him as the key witness, the case against Webber fell apart. He pleaded guilty to a lesser charge to avoid prison time, paid a fine, did some community service, and walked away clean. It's fair to say that nobody benefitted more from the timing of Ed Martin's death than Chris Webber.

It absolutely blows my mind that Chris now does analysis and color commentary on national television for NBA TV and TNT, looking quite cool and carefree. His 10-year ban from the University of Michigan is over, and he was considered for induction into the Naismith Memorial Basketball Hall of Fame in 2017. The Hall of Freakin' Fame. I heard him say on NBA TV not long ago, "I love doing things that have never been done before." Well, ain't that the truth.

Neither Chris Webber nor his parents attended Dad's funeral service. After all Ed had done for them. And they weren't the only no-shows, not by a long shot. Mitch Albom, the nationally-known sports columnist for the *Detroit Free Press*, wrote an article about Ed's funeral; I assume he was there, because he certainly made note of who was not:

> "They say you can measure your life by those who attend your funeral. But in the case of 69-year-old Ed Martin... it was those who did not attend that told the story.
>
> "Where was Chris Webber? Where was Jalen Rose? Where was Maurice Taylor or Robert Traylor or the other NBA-caliber basketball players that Martin helped, players he so wanted to please, offering everything from rides to birthday cakes to hundreds of thousands of dollars? Where were all these players who admitted to taking his money because he was a 'good, caring man,' just trying to help them out?
>
> "Where were they when it was time to say good-bye?

"They were elsewhere, earning their millions, because that is what happens with players and boosters; when the latter are no longer needed, they often are no longer wanted."

I was told Jalen Rose wasn't there, but his mother, Jeannie, was. That's a perfect representation of their relationship: Jalen wanted to distance himself from Ed as much as possible, yet his mother felt the need to be there in order to show respect for what he'd done.

I understand that Antoine Joubert, "The Judge" – was at the funeral, too. The dominating guard who was named Michigan's "Mr. Basketball" at Detroit's Southwestern High School the year after my father made himself the best friend of the program and its head coach, Perry Watson. However, he hung out way in the back. Antoine felt an obligation to pay his respects, but he didn't want anybody asking him about his relationship with Ed.

Honestly, though, these were things I was told. For the most part, I really don't remember who was there and who was not. The enormous sanctuary was maybe half full, and I vaguely recall accepting condolences from a lot of people and shaking many hands. But so much of that day was a blur, even at the time. I was in a very guarded emotional state. I would call it "quiet turmoil." You probably couldn't see it in my face, and you definitely couldn't tell what was going on inside my head. I couldn't take my eyes off that casket. And my mind was racing in so many different directions.

I was extremely concerned about my mother and her feelings, both physical and emotional. Hilda Martin was somewhere between profound grief and shock. She had to be thinking, How dare you leave this earth before me like this! Here I am, the one who's sick and fighting for my life, and you just check out of here and leave me to fend for myself?

From my perspective, we didn't lack for anything from my father. There was always plenty of money around when I was growing up and we had everything we needed from a material standpoint. But Dad's love of those dollars and his need to be out chasing them, combined with his unlimited generosity, meant he was away from home a great deal.

Another thing about Dad – he had an obsessive personality. For years he spent a lot of time – too much time, Mom would say – at the racetrack. In validation of my mother's point, at one time my dad had private boxes (similar to a suite at a football stadium) at Windsor Raceway, the DRC (Detroit Race Course), and Hazel Park Raceway, and he attended Northville Downs occasionally. Then he replaced that passion with basketball, concentrating his focus on Southwestern High School. Mom had to share him with all his varied pursuits, and then at the time she needed him most... he was gone again. This time he was gone for good.

Then there was my brother, Bruce. At the time, he was staying in the Caro Center, the state mental health hospital in Caro, Michigan. As a young adult, he was originally diagnosed with schizophrenia and it was later changed to bipolar disorder. Hospital staffers brought him down to Detroit for the funeral – flanking him on either side, accompanying him everywhere he went. He arrived in his facility clothes, wearing a long leather coat, and changed into his suit in the pastor's office.

Suddenly, Bruce realized he couldn't find his dress shoes, either because he misplaced them or didn't bring them from Caro in the first place. We needed to find him a replacement pair, and quickly so he wouldn't have to wear his raggedly old shoes from the hospital to his father's funeral. He said, "I want a pair of Dad's shoes," and since his feet always were considerably bigger than mine, we didn't have many options. Someone was dispatched to our father's house to retrieve a pair of dress shoes for my brother.

When the Oxfords arrived, he looked up at me as he slipped them on. "You know," he said, "I was never able to walk in his shoes."

We shared a chuckle over that, but I'm sure he was having a

real moment, putting on his father's shoes to attend his funeral. I hoped he could handle the emotions of this day, because he was dealing with so many other things inside his head.

As I stared at that coffin I remember thinking, "I can hear Dad talking to me. I know what he would say if he was here: "You have to be strong now for your mother. You have to be strong for your brother." I felt like I had to try and keep up a façade of strength, so they would know they could lean on me for support.

It was a curious mix of congregants at the church. There were present and former Ford employees, family members, athletes, fellow railbirds from the local racetrack, and people representing others who decided it was prudent not to be there. I'm certain there were workers and acquaintances from his second and more lucrative career, running the policy racket on the streets of Detroit. I'm sure most of them had one question in the back of their minds, the same question a church elder asked the congregation during the ceremony: "Who do you think Eddie Martin was?"

Greater New Mt. Moriah Missionary Baptist was not my father's church. It was the home church of my wife, Robin, who had attended there since she was a girl. Ed Martin was not the kind of guy to have a home church. He didn't frequent them, but he attended several, including the church I grew up in, Divine Congregational Church of God in Christ. And, either because he wanted to deepen his ties to the Webbers to stay close to Chris or because he genuinely liked the family, he was a frequent guest at Rosedale Park Baptist Church where Chris's father served as deacon.

However, Greater New Mt. Moriah held a special connection for my father because of its pastor, The Rev. Kenneth J. Flowers. Ed knew Pastor Flowers well, but his church had little to do with it: his home shared a driveway with my mother's older sister, my Aunt Lillian. My father confided many things to my aunt, so he would see Flowers several times a week when he went to visit her.

Like so many others in Ed's wide circle of acquaintances,

Rev. Flowers was a beneficiary of his boundless spirit of giving. Ed would stop by his house often with cakes, ice cream and other treats, just by virtue of his home's proximity to my aunt's house.

He also believed that if you were going to buy something, you should get the best. Example: When Ed brought Rev. Flowers ice cream, he wouldn't just stop by Farmer Jack and pick up a pint. He would make the fifty-mile round trip drive to Northville, Michigan, to the family-owned Guernsey Farms, and bring back a rich, creamy half-gallon. It got to the point, Rev. Flowers recalled, that he would plead, "Ed, I'm on a diet. I can't keep eating all of these cakes and sweets." But Dad was relentless with his deliveries. And my God, that ice cream was good.

Rev. Flowers delivered Ed's eulogy, and while some pastors have to improvise in making home-going remarks for people who weren't church members, Rev. Flowers knew my father so well that his comments were specific and quite personal. "Although I didn't see him a lot in church," he said, "I saw him a lot next door to me."

People I've spoken to recall that Rev. Flowers cautioned the congregation not to believe everything they read in the papers about Ed Martin. It's acceptable for white people to exploit our young inner-city youths through various means, he noted, not the least of which is using their bodies and athletic abilities for the benefit of colleges and universities. While Ed has been vilified, Rev. Flowers emphasized, it was important to note that he reached out and helped black kids instead of exploiting them. Maybe that's one reason he was so controversial, Flowers suggested, because you didn't see black men doing that very often – and institutions didn't appreciate the competition.

Though he cautioned FBI agents not to appear, Attorney Bill Mitchell got up and spoke that day. He said he very seldom attended the funerals of his clients, and was even less likely to shed a tear over their passing. But he did both where Ed was concerned because he considered my father more of a friend than anything else. Actually, they met years before at the racetrack where they shared a common passion, so the relationship they developed was far different than your basic lawyer-client association.

Mitchell liked Ed. He respected Ed. And he seemed genuinely moved by his death. And he made sure to tell the story about the agents' request.

A succession of other people stood up, walked to a microphone and said a few words in remembrance. Most of what they said has been lost to time. But of all the people I spoke to, nobody has forgotten what Jessie Mae Carter said that day.

Jessie Mae was the grandmother of Robert "Tractor" Traylor, the 6-foot-7, 320-pound, enormously talented player who starred at the University of Michigan and went on to a seven-year career in the pros. Ed had become close to Traylor while the latter was still at Murray-Wright High School, elevating a team that had won only two games the year before his arrival to the state Class A championship in his junior year. Traylor went on to become Michigan's Mr. Basketball as a senior, but his life outside school was hardly as glittering.

His mother was a drug addict, so he lived mostly with his grandmother, Jessie Mae Carter, in a cramped three-bedroom house on Detroit's west side that they also shared with his aunt and his brother. Jessie Mae supported the family as best she could with her work as a janitor, but it was a hand-to-mouth existence.

In Traylor, Eddie saw some of the same outsized skills he had admired in Webber. He saw a player who could be a huge boon to a U-M program that became the next focal point for my dad after Southwestern High. However, he also saw a young man who too often seemed overwhelmed by crushing poverty. Tractor Traylor had managed to steer clear of the drugs, crime and the worst of what the streets of Detroit had to offer, but Ed worried about how desperation might impact his future.

For my father, Tractor's situation was irresistible. Shortly after befriending him, Dad was paying regular visits to Jessie Mae's home, dropping off groceries, appliances and, of course, plenty of cash. By the time Robert graduated from Murray-Wright in 1995 and made his way to Ann Arbor to play for the Wolverines, visits to and from Ed had become routine. And even though it was Robert's knock on Ed's front door the night of February 16, 1996, that ultimately led to the downfall of Ed's financial enterprise, the bond between the two was strong and genuine.

Perhaps wisely, Traylor didn't show up for the funeral. He probably wanted to avoid the scrutiny, and he wasn't a guy who could easily hide in the shadows. But he would have been more than welcome. Of all the high-school players who asked my father for additional assistance, Robert was the only one who repaid every nickel Ed had given him once he began making his millions in the NBA.

However, Jessie Mae had enough to say for Tractor and the entire family. An imposing presence like her grandson, she didn't approach the microphone: at 6-foot-3, 270 pounds, she didn't need to. She commanded attention simply by standing up. Besides, her aching knees impeded her from moving more than she absolutely had to.

She faced the crowd from her pew and spoke, loudly and clearly. "It's important for me to say Ed Martin was a great man," Jessie Mae boomed. "I know two things: There were many days I would not have been able to put food on the table if it hadn't been for Ed Martin. And if it wasn't for Ed Martin, Robert Traylor would never have become a pro basketball player. That's how important he was to my family."

Her voice grew even louder. "I don't give a damn what people say! What anybody says! I know he was a good man!"

When a respected mother figure of the neighborhood stands up and cusses in the middle of church, people tend to remember what she said.

When the funeral was over, I don't think many people knew any more about Ed Martin than they did before. Everybody who came to the services that day brought their own opinion about the man, and the emotions of the ceremony and his burial at Woodlawn Cemetery on Woodward Avenue probably did little to change anyone's mind. I'm sure of this, though: there are many alumni and fans of the University of Michigan who think they know where Ed is today. They believed he wore horns and a tail while he was living.

Ultimately, unintentionally, my father's actions led to a six-year NCAA investigation of U-M and its men's basketball program; subsequent investigations by the FBI, IRS and Department of Justice; caused the firing of head coach Steve Fisher; and brought four years of NCAA probation. It left in its wake for U-M the loss of scholarships and the vacating of Michigan's 1997 National Invitation Tournament championship, 1998 Big Ten Tournament crown and its 1992 and 1993 Final Four appearances.

I'm sure there are few Wolverines' faithful who couldn't hate my father any more if he had climbed to the top of Crisler Arena, the home court of Michigan basketball, and ripped down those banners with his own hands. And with more than 540,000 living University of Michigan alums, one of the largest alumni bodies in the world, that's a lot of hate.

CHAPTER TWO

Hustle Play

I can't hear or read the year 2003 without it flashing in my mind that was when my father died. It always sparks a question I have heard so many times from friends and strangers alike:

"Why, after all this time, did you decide to write a book? Ed Martin has been gone for so long, his misdeeds as well as his kind and generous deeds are things of the past. Why not let the man and his memory rest in peace?"

Legitimate questions.

Some cynics have accused me of trying to capitalize on the enduring legend and popularity of the University of Michigan's Fab Five – Juwan Howard, Ray Jackson, Jimmy King, Jalen Rose and Chris Webber. To this day that quintet stands as the most celebrated – and notorious – recruiting class in college basketball history. I can see how that might look like my motivation. People are entitled to their own opinions. But a motive of exploitation could not be further from the truth.

Yes, it would have been sweet if this book's release had coincided with the March 2011 premiere of the *Fab Five* documentary that was broadcast on ESPN. We were working on the manuscript long before that. Surely we would have caught a wave of free publicity and been swept along on the buzz of an eagerly anticipated and heavily promoted national telecast.

But this book wasn't ready then, not even close. When the

documentary aired, I had already been on a personal mission for many years to finish this project. I had been through a couple of veteran ghostwriters, plowed through a mountain of edits, sifted through months of interviews, transcriptions, records and notes, and burned through a pile of dollars. Throughout, I was certain that one day it would be worth it to have the work completed, to have delivered on a solemn promise. But that day was still off somewhere in the future.

It would be years until I could make good on a promise made to my mother as she faced the last days of her life.

Hilda Martin, my mother, had been fighting lung cancer for some time when Ed passed away. Stricken with her own terminal illness, in the face of her husband's death, she must have felt abandoned, angry, weak and grief-stricken, perhaps all at the same time.

It was not the first time she had felt that way.

Mom was an extremely private person. Many of my father's activities were conducted against her wishes. She told him repeatedly not to expect any of the people on whom he lavished money and presents to be there for him if he ever needed a hand. She suggested that if he really cared about his family and the many kids he supported over the years, he would be more secretive about his gifts and about where he got the money that made them possible.

If her words of caution even registered with Ed after so many years of marriage, he gave them little heed.

At first, even the thought of having a book like this written, as Ed and I had discussed only superficially prior to his death, caused my mother dismay. An honest book meant that long-buried family secrets would be dug up and exposed.

Quite a shock, then, when she summoned me to her bedside to talk about just such a book even as her cancer was in the final stages.

Mom said Ed deserved to have the full story told. She meant the story of Ed Martin's sincere concern for the kids he tried to help, a generosity not limited to the superstar players but rather extending to the last kid on the bench. It was more than the gifts, more than the money. It was how he showed youngsters the kind of hands-on guidance he himself never received as a boy.

Mom felt that only I could truly do the story justice. Even though I was his son, she believed I would neither romanticize Ed's actions nor vilify them, as had been done by so many in the media and the public who never met this man.

"Clear his name by telling the truth," she said, staring into my eyes. "The full story, good and otherwise. You have to change the image that the world has about your father."

I promised that I would.

A few days after that brief conversation, Mom made another trip to the hospital and was admitted. She never came home again. That promise became the driving force for me to see this book through.

Like all sons have done, I'm sure I let my mother down at times. I wasn't about to do it again.

But how to begin telling the full Ed Martin story, rough bark and all, unvarnished?

In Chapter One, we looked backward from his funeral and recapped some of the obvious high and low points of his life and introduced the major players.

But those things had long since been written about over and over again, almost invariably treated superficially and sensationalized. If one really wants to understand who this infamous booster was and why and how he did what he did, then you have to get past the façade. You need to expose the man behind the curtain.

In the life of Ed Martin there are many surprising and unremarked mileposts along the way. There was a poor, stifling upbringing in rural Georgia, an environment that easily could have crushed his spirit and destroyed his potential. There was his Great Migration to Detroit, a land of opportunity for black men, and his subsequent career at Ford.

Any full account of Ed Martin's life has to answer the basic question of how did this hourly factory worker get the money to pay for his lavish generosity. The following chapters will do that. We'll cover Ed's foray into the numbers business, his rise to emerge as one of the most successful illegal lottery operators in Detroit (before the Michigan State Lottery emerged to become his major competition), and see the inner workings of his illicit numbers operation. There are many stones to be turned over, including the genesis of his relationship with Southwestern High School and its legendary head coach, Perry Watson. It was the all-consuming Martin-Watson liaison that sowed the first seeds for the ultimate downfall of Ed Martin.

Yes, we'll get to all that, and more.

But first, let's focus on the likely reason you are reading this book: to get the inside skinny on Ed Martin's association with the two biggest names in this saga:

Chris Webber and Jalen Rose.

Ironically, Ed's closest connection with any kid other than my brother and me was with the best player Southwestern High ever recruited but couldn't land: Chris Webber. Ed first saw Webber and Rose in 1987, when both were eighth graders. I'm certain of that because Ed raced home to tell me about them after the first time he watched them play at the PAL (Police Athletic League) gymnasium.

Just turned 14 years old, the two were teammates on an AAU summer league team called the "Superfriends" that was the buzz of the city. Ed remembered seeing future Southwestern High stand-

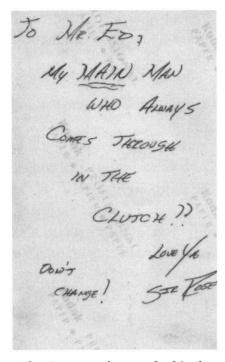 

Jalen Rose was known for his sharp moves, in the game or out on the town

out and NBA shooting guard Voshon Lenard there, among others, but Rose and Webber clearly were kings of the court.

These games between junior high school-aged teens had become can't-miss events, packing the bleachers with incredulous fans as well as high school recruiters who were practically drooling at the mouth. They knew that landing just one of the two could be enough to set their team on a straight path to a state hoops title.

Rose was already tougher than most Detroit high school guards, with a relentless drive, deft shooting touch, and court awareness embedded in his genes: his biological father was the former NBA No.1 draft pick and longtime Detroit Pistons guard, the late Jimmy Walker. He seemed like a lock to attend Southwestern High. Rose had grown up in northwest Detroit and was raised on the roundball exploits of Bill Jones, Leslie Rockymore and Antoine Joubert.

Ed Martin could see this kid was a "Southwestern guy" through and through even before he donned the uniform.

Southwestern's coach Perry Watson had known Jalen since he was a youth. He was practically born to play for Perry. And that sat fine with my father, who had focused his obsessive nature on Southwestern years earlier after discovering that his Ford co-worker, Zeke Joubert, was Antoine's dad.

Ed had no other initial connection to Southwestern other than the Jouberts. He wasn't a graduate, had no kids of his own at the school, didn't even live near that part of Detroit. Yet, he fashioned himself as the team's biggest fan, reveled in its rise to greatness in the Detroit Public School League (PSL), and made himself an intimate friend of Coach Watson.

Along the way, Ed supported the team any way he could. That included frequent "cash handshakes" in the locker room and paying the utility bills and other expenses for players' families in need. The fact that Jalen, one of the city's most exciting young players, was ticketed for Southwestern made Big Ed giddy.

Chris Webber, however, was another matter entirely. Literally head and shoulders above other ballers his age, Chris also stood taller than many of his coaches, a freakishly gifted physical specimen. As good as Rose was, and no one disputed his remarkable natural gifts, Webber was undeniably better. As my father told me:

> *I went down there to see teams play. I hadn't seen Chris Webber play before. I told Perry I was going down to take a look at him. And I said to myself, 'Look at that guy! He's stronger and he's playing harder! Darn, boy, he's something else!'*

Jalen was sharp, too. He was good. But even back then, going into ninth grade, he was no Chris Webber. I could see it! Chris was bigger than everybody, he could dunk the ball, he could dribble the ball. He was just pure raw talent. He had a very rough swagger, undeveloped, but it was still swagger. I was sitting in the stands, just in disbelief at Webber. I could tell he was going to be better than the rest.

That's all Dad needed to see. He revered excellence, and he envisioned himself as Southwestern High's unofficial, volunteer recruiter. The thought of seeing both Webber and Rose flying to the basket in the blue and gold of the Southwestern Prospectors made him almost salivate.

What's more, it seemed doable. The two players had developed a bond both on and off the court. They came from wildly divergent backgrounds – Rose, poor and fatherless in the 'hood after Walker deserted them, raised by the streets and a single mother; Webber, the son of an autoworker father and a schoolteacher mom. Webber's parents were both church deacons and raised their son in a solid middle-class household. As can happen with kids from different backgrounds, basketball became the common ground upon which the two established a friendship. Rose and Webber had already developed such chemistry together that some observers speculated that Webber would follow his buddy Rose to Southwestern.

No such fantasizing for Ed Martin. He set a goal of making it happen. The colossal talents of Webber and Rose combined would almost guarantee a state title – and maybe more than one. Heady stuff for the ultimate booster.

As Ed Martin let these visions of basketball glory dance in his head while watching the "Superfriends" dominate, he felt a nudge from a nearby fan.

"That's his father over there," the fan said, pointing to a tall man standing on the gymnasium floor.

Naturally, Dad wasted no time. He stepped down to the floor to introduce himself, turning on the Big Ed charm. "Mr. Webber," he said, "Boy, your son can really play!"

Mayce Webber (after whom Chris is named: his full name

is Mayce Edward Christopher Webber III) smiled and laughed, beaming with that pride a father displays when others boast about his son's abilities. Ed remembered thinking, "I wouldn't mind getting involved with that situation, because I really enjoyed Chris's style. My thing was to try to get him to go to Southwestern."

Mayce introduced Ed to Chris. The two men talked a bit, then exchanged phone numbers, and Ed said he would call. "'Come by my house', that's the way he put it," Ed said. "Come and see Chris play a lot more."

Ed Martin had seen all he really needed to in order to judge the talent and the enormous potential of Chris Webber. But he would indeed take Mayce up on his offer to "come by the house" and to "come and see Chris play a lot more." As with any truly effective booster, Ed needed a means to get close to the family so he could begin his campaign to recruit this phenomenally gifted talent to Southwestern High School.

What he couldn't foresee was the daunting uphill battle he would have to wage. Chris' mother, Doris, had fallen in love with Detroit Country Day School, an elite private academy located in the chichi suburb of Beverly Hills, north of Detroit. An educator herself, Doris was far more concerned with her son's GPA than his points per game, and by comparison the Detroit public school system left much to be desired.

What's more, Country Day was more than willing to offer the Webbers a full-ride scholarship, no small enticement since tuition at the school in the 1980s was well over $10,000 a year.

The way Ed put it:

I knew Southwestern Coach Perry Watson liked Jalen because he heard that Chris was already committed to Country Day, and he wasn't going to come to Southwestern. Ain't no way his mother would let him come to Southwestern. She controlled all that. That's what I heard through the grapevine.

Not that reality would deter Ed from his mission. He told Watson he was prepared to do whatever it took to win Webber for Southwestern High. Watson told him to back off: sure, he would have loved to have Chris on his team, but it was clear to him Webber was heading to Country Day and that was that. Watson wasn't about to beg any kid to come to Southwestern, no matter how rare a talent he was.

That didn't dissuade Big Ed. He was determined to put on his own full-court press.

Soon after – in the summer of 1987 – Chris attended classes at Country Day to ensure he would be admitted for the fall semester. Though Ed saw little value in making the trip other than "putting his face in the place," Ed took the long drive out to Country Day to watch him play even though, astonishingly, when organized games began, Chris wasn't starting.

Ed had also been attending the church where the Webbers served as deacons, Rosedale Park Baptist Church. And he visited the Webber's home enough times to be easily mistaken for the family's rich uncle. "I sat up there with him a thousand times before he went and enrolled in Country Day," he recalled, "trying to get him to come to Southwestern and play for Coach Perry with some of these other guys."

Meanwhile, Ed began reading articles about Michael Jordan, already on his way to NBA immortality since joining the Chicago Bulls three seasons earlier. "He was playing pretty good there," Ed understated. "I was reading how much he was making, the endorsements, all the things he could do and what have you, and I said, 'Boy, Chris could be another Michael Jordan!'"

So that is when Ed Martin's obsessive nature shifted focus from Chris Webber to a new target: the Webber family. In his own words:

Deacon [Mayce] Webber and I started talking. He needed a few things and I started helping him get those things. And there was no resentment there. I helped Chris do a LOT of things.

I made sure he had spending money, every week, starting from there. It was the same with Jalen. But it wasn't no big money all the time with Jalen. I used to make sure they got 10 or 20 dollars a week, something like that. You know, I don't even count that.

Chris? I went by his house every day, almost. I'd stop by on my way home. And I made sure he had food, his family had food. I made sure they had fruit, bacon. Every Saturday I'd shop. When I bought ours, I'd buy theirs. Matter of fact, I brought them so much food, Mrs. Webber told me the freezer was too full, to stop buying 'cause she had too much for Chris, his three younger brothers and his younger sister.

If Chris needed something, I made it where Deacon Webber could get it. Like if he needed shoes, shorts – matter of fact, if Deacon Webber just said they didn't give him this or that, I would give him a couple pairs of shoes. And I hooked it up where eventually they could go to Blackburn's (a former Detroit clothing store) and get what they want, more or less. They'd sign, and then I'd pay for it.

If Chris would need something, I'd make sure he had some money. If he'd say, 'I need twenty,' I'd give it to him. He didn't want to deal drugs or nothing like that, he just didn't have no money.

Once he sprained his ankle and I went and got him plastic supports. Whatever Chris needed, I tried to get. I looked for shoes; he wore a size 17, 18. I bought him a pair of loafers, another pair of shoes you lace. Then I made sure he had suits, clothes. I got him three of four thousand dollars' worth of stuff from out there at Jack's Place (a suburban Detroit men's store). Another day, he got four or five thousand dollars' worth of stuff. Then, a lot of things he'd sign for and I bought them.

I just started taking care of him and made sure he had money every day. And if there was anything he needed, I gave it to him.

It appeared that Ed's efforts had paid off. Chris Webber did indeed enroll at Southwestern and Perry Watson was assigned to be his counselor.

Yet, any chance Webber still might be persuaded to forsake his Country Day scholarship for Southwestern quickly vanished because of a development unforeseen and beyond Ed Martin's control. After six months of negotiations failed, the Detroit Federation of Teachers went on strike in September of 1987. That dashed Ed Martin's dream of a Webber-Rose duo at Southwestern because Doris Webber, devoted mom and sympathetic teacher, never would have allowed her son to begin his freshman year under such tenuous circumstances.

Still, the Ed Martin gravy train rolled on. Even though Mayce Webber was gainfully employed, same as my dad, it seemed that the Webbers always had a need they couldn't handle themselves, and Ed the Booster was happy to oblige. Over the next several years, he would provide the Webber family with expensive meals, trips, home appliances, and cash. Big Ed had become so close to Chris, in fact, that he often referred to himself as Webber's "godfather." And for good reason, as he described it:

His godfather had passed, and I said, 'Well, maybe that's a good job for me!' I asked his mother and father, and they said, 'Yeah.' They told me I could be his godfather, 'cause his godfather had passed. And the godfather does a lot of things for kids. So, I was happy about that.

Dad bought Chris his high school class ring, talked a girl into being his date for prom, paid for his graduation party, and booked hotel suites for him and his buddies to get wild at places like the

Following up on the money trail, Ed Martin would pay off the tab at Blackburn Clothing and other stores, for Jalen Rose and other players

The 1991 Southwestern High School team celebrated minutes after winning the state championship in Michigan. This Prospector powerhouse squad also was ranked Number 1 in the country and featured Jalen Rose, standing in the back row, next to the left shoulder of the tall player in the center; Flinn Hall, number 24, standing at the left; Voshon Lenard, kneeling at the lower right; and Carlton King, in the middle of the photo, with the high-top haircut. Other teammates were Dannie Hayes, Derrick Hayes, Carlton King, Quincy Bowen, Ike Gamble, Ibn Bakari, Dee Wilkerson, Michael Hamilton, Kamau Alexander, Randy Steele. Managers were: Darryl Tarplin, Michael Dotson. Coaching the team were head coach Perry Watson; assistant coaches Herman, Blake, and Majors.

Ritz-Carlton and the Hyatt Regency. Ed Martin became Chris Webber's personal ATM.

And to this day the question lingers: Why? Why did Ed go so overboard in so many ways for Chris and his family? I believe there was some genuine affection there, that he really grew to love the Webbers, but it had to be more than that. You love a lot of people and don't engulf them with money and gifts.

Did he want to get deep into the inner circle of a great basketball player who had the potential to excel in college and as a pro? Was he making an investment for his own future? I know for a fact that Chris told him frequently, and in no uncertain terms, that when he "made it big," he would pay Ed back for everything. Every gift. Every "cash withdrawal." Ed said with pride:

Oh, it's so many things I did for Chris. I tried to show him things, do things that he'd never done. I was more like his mentor. I really loved Chris! I thought – and I'm not going to lie about it – there's a helluva chance for me to get somewhere! And he, you know, promising he'd take care of me, pay it back...

A spoiled, entitled, supremely gifted man-child crossed paths with a star-struck, compulsive, deep-pocketed benefactor. It was a toxic mix.

Ironically, Southwestern didn't need Webber's services: by the 1990-91 season, the senior year for Jalen Rose and Voshon Lenard, the Prospectors were Michigan Class A state champions for the second consecutive year and ranked the No. 1 high school team in America.

CHAPTER THREE

Training Days

In the summer of 1999, after our homes had been raided by the FBI, IRS and other federal alphabet combinations, Dad and I were negotiating plea deals.

He was being hounded so relentlessly by the media in search of in-depth interviews that he felt like a hunted man. So, when Lisa Mathis, a filmmaker from California and the sister of a friend, arrived in Michigan to visit family, he had a quick answer to her question. She asked if she could interview Ed and me for a possible documentary on the scandal. His immediate response was, "Uh, no. I'm not doing that."

I wasn't so quick to reject the idea out of hand, however. In fact, after some consideration, I decided to let Lisa interview me – as a favor to my friend, and also to gain some firsthand experience with the process. I'd never interviewed anybody before. The way she interviewed me was essentially the format I would later use to interview Dad and everyone else who participated with this book.

She set up a camera in the rec room of my house, sat across from me and conducted my interview. I probably paid more attention to the questions and the way she phrased them than I did to my answers. When it was over, I felt like a patient walking out of his dentist's office: "Hey, that didn't hurt as much as I thought it would." From a creative standpoint, the experience with Lisa was a godsend.

Fast forward to 2002.

I still didn't have any concrete plans to write a book, but something compelled me to get my father's story down and preserved in some fashion. He wasn't going to tell his own story. I figured he would sit down and do an interview with me, and I knew he sure as hell wouldn't do one with anybody else. Who better than me to be his Bryant Gumbel?

I mean, you live with the man every day because he's your father, but how many of us ever sit down and ask, "Dad, what's your story? I want to know more about you. Start at the beginning, and give me all the detail you can." If we were smart enough to do that, we would capture and hold a lot more knowledge about our parents, our families…and ourselves.

We hadn't decided to do a book at this stage. Hadn't even talked about it, really. But I had an encounter years earlier, before heading to do 13 months in a Pennsylvania prison camp, that definitely got my thoughts moving in that direction. And with a year and one month under confinement, I had plenty of time to think about it more.

I remember thinking Dad is 69 years old. Nobody had any way of knowing he wouldn't live to see 70. Most of the life he once lived with such outsized flair and flamboyant passion is gone now. You can hear it in his voice: clear but gravelly, heavy, weary, as if weighed down from years of unrelenting stress and turmoil.

I put to use the interview skills Lisa had used on me years before. She began by asking me for my background, essentially encouraging me to tell my life story, so that's how I started with Dad.

I turned on the tape recorder and we sat down at the table. He gave me that look – the one that Ernie Harwell used to call the "family look." You know, the one fathers give their sons when they can't quite figure out what the hell their kid is doing.

"OK," I began, "could you state your name for the purposes of this recording?"

As Dad replied, he looked more than a bit uneasy.

My name is Eddie L. Martin. I was born in Alpharetta, Georgia, January 17, 1934.

Back then, the way it was usually done, I was probably born at home. I don't remember Alpharetta because we moved to Roswell, Georgia, when I was real young. Roswell was 21 miles from Atlanta... 19, maybe. I went to Roswell Elementary School. I had the normal lifestyle of a kid born in a country life.

We weren't rich, but we weren't poor, either. We was average. We might have been one step above average from what other people had out there. My mom worked all the time, and my stepfather worked all the time.

No one who understands where Dad came from wonders where he acquired his work ethic. He was the fourth of five children born to Hattie Stafford, a small-town veterans' hospital employee with an impressive entrepreneurial streak and an unquenchable drive that he and his siblings had to observe and absorb.

Hattie left Dad's biological father not long after he was born, fed up with his heavy drinking. She married Samuel Stafford a few years later, a talented chef who worked in many of the finer restaurants in and around predominantly white Roswell.

My dad, Charles Martin, left Georgia and moved up here [Detroit]. He was supposed to come back and get us. But he never did.

In addition to her full-time duties at the hospital and any odd jobs she could pick up, Hattie teamed with her second husband to plant a for-profit vegetable farm on their land, operate a boarding house and even run a "juke joint" – really more community center than rowdy late-night hangout, a space where locals could gather for a smoke and a soda while listening to the latest tunes on the jukebox. She was teaching by example.

Hattie never had to preach to Eddie about the value of determination, hustle or sweat on one's brow. Her simultaneous ventures showed him the importance of keeping a laser-like focus on your bottom line and doing whatever you have to do to maintain it.

And she kept her multiple enterprises going long after Ed left home. I remember even during my childhood summer visits south, I would always see my grandmother had some kind of money-making operation going on in her backyard or her basement or somewhere else on her acre and a half of farmland.

The very young Ed Martin and his mother, Hattie

She had three bedrooms, at least. She only occupied one, then she put an addition on her house that gave her another whole one. It was a nice little hookup.

I remember the basement door always had a lock on it. If you walked out onto the patio – she had a nice cement patio – and down the steps, now you're at the back of the house, which was like a whole 'nother world. That's where the boarders would go in. She had people staying with her. They paid her rent.

She also grew crops. She would farm her land, do it all herself, raise the corn. I remember she had two deep freezers, Kenmores, with locks on them, and they would be just packed with clear containers with all these vegetables. She would grow them, sell them, can and preserve them.

She was almost like a mother figure to these boarders

she had. She sold cigarettes and pop to them. I'd help her sometimes, even though she never let me sell cigarettes. They'd come, you know, and say, 'I need an orange soda,' so I would go to the freezer or the refrigerator wherever it was and get them the soda.

She was always a hardworking woman – a real, you know, entrepreneur.

For his part, my grandfather, Charles Martin, decided he'd be better off seeking his fortune in the industrialized North. That was the Promised Land to black Southerners in that era: high-wage, low-skill jobs were plentiful and the crushing weight of Jim Crow far less oppressive. Charles moved to Detroit in the late 1930s and promised Hattie that, once he got settled, he'd send for his children. Meanwhile, Eddie followed in his mother's work boots.

I began to work at 10, 12. I worked for 10 cents an hour, helping build houses and helping on the farm or picking cotton, those regular things you do in a rural area. I worked all the time. I'd work 10 hours a day in summer. I used to make $1 a day, and I was happy. We picked cotton on Saturdays when I was in school to make extra money.

Before Charles could send for Ed, however, Hattie shipped him and his brother Bob off to Detroit anyway, to live with her sister, Mattie Gwinn, in the predominantly Polish-American enclave of Hamtramck.

As driven as she was, my grandmother finally had become overwhelmed with juggling work and child rearing around the clock. Hattie prayed her sister could provide some relief. Plus, she desperately wanted more for her children than the hardscrabble, hand-to-mouth existence she endured in Roswell. She hoped Ed and Bob would have an easier time outside the segregated South.

Ed Martin fell in love with Detroit the moment his feet hit the concrete. The bustle and buzz of big city life captivated him. He had seen Atlanta, but only through car windows; now he felt like a real city dweller. His aunt took him along with the family on day trips to downtown movie theaters and to Belle Isle, a sprawling island park nestled off the banks of the Detroit River.

In school at Hamtramck, Ed proved to be a precocious student who excelled at a number of subjects. Yet, even in this more competitive new environment, he astonished them at math. He could work out an equation in his head faster than any of his schoolmates – faster even than some of his teachers. He said he did so well so quickly in Hamtramck, the administration decided to promote him by two grades. In a matter of weeks, he was moved from fifth to seventh grade.

His glory days in Detroit didn't last long, however. Hattie had planned to come to Detroit and join her sons but unexpectedly became really sick. So, just months after they left Roswell, Ed and Bob returned home to Roswell to care for her.

Dad wouldn't soon forget his brief taste of urban life, though. In fact, he could think about little else upon his return to rural Georgia. Detroit's wide streets, the palpable energy, the ceaseless hum of motion – they captivated him. Ed Martin was born a small-town boy, but somehow he knew he was cut out for brighter lights, bigger things. He knew that eventually, he'd be back to the Motor City for more.

When Ed returned to Georgia, he also returned to the workforce.

> *I hopped cars at the drive-in. I made a lot of money there. Sometimes I'd be waiting on 20 cars at a time, 25, working for tips and whatever. I did that well. That was mostly in high school. I did that and had to go to high school. A man would come around and take 10 or 12 of us, as many as he could pack into a station wagon, and we went to high school in Atlanta.*

It certainly wasn't Dad's choice to travel 20 miles each way to high school five days a week. There was a high school in Roswell. But Roswell High was segregated, whites only, and the racist realities of the times meant that Ed and other black children in the town were jammed into raggedy old cars – of course, there were no school buses – and shuttled to Atlanta's Booker T. Washington High, nearly an hour's drive away.

The high school in my area only accepted whites. Blacks couldn't go to it at that time. I could almost throw a rock from my house to the school… but we couldn't go.

My father never forgot the sting of segregation. Really, how could anyone? And I don't think he ever forgot the rage and indignity he felt at the blatant unfairness of denying any group of people – especially children – the same opportunities others enjoyed not because of something they had done, but because of antiquated, unjust rules. I believe Ed's seething anger over that hypocrisy haunted him well into his adult years, and influenced many of the choices he made.

Despite all that, however, Ed said he recalled his experience at Booker T. High as overwhelmingly positive.

We had all the regular things that a school should have. We had shop. We had homecoming queens. I played trumpet in a marching band. We marched at football games. You know, regular stuff.

Outgoing and talkative, Dad made friends easily among both students and teachers. And while he preferred band to sports teams, it's said that he wasn't a bad athlete, often seen playing in pickup softball and football games around Roswell. His heavy-set, 5-foot-10 frame probably could have earned Ed a spot on one of Booker T.'s teams, but even then his true interest in sports tended more toward cheering and admiring talent than organized participation. He was content to sit in the bleachers at his school's basketball games, rooting wildly for his classmates.

His true skills continued to stand out in the classroom. Ed's

The Booster 35

name was a fixture on the high school's honor roll – even when he couldn't resist the temptation to make some mischief.

I made one 'D' while I was in school. And that's because I was talkin', runnin' off at the mouth. I was devilish. I'd shoot spitballs and do like the rest of the kids in class. The teacher gave me a 'D.' She said that was fair. She gave me that 'D' trying to make me improve. I never got another one.

He read voraciously and excelled in a variety of subjects, but his gift for numbers had grown even sharper. Whether it was basic math or complex trigonometry, Ed could work out even the most complicated problems in half the time of many of his peers.

In fact, one of my favorite memories as a kid was going into supermarkets around Detroit with my dad. We'd shop for our groceries and put them all on the conveyor belt. Now remember, there were no electronic scanners or computerized cash registers at that time: every item had a price stamped on it, and each one had to be rung up individually.

Well, no matter how many items we had on the belt, be it two or 72, Ed would calculate the cost of each product as it rolled by, add in the tax, and announce the grand total to the cashier before she even touched the last product! I never saw him fail: He'd add up the prices, give the correct figure to the penny, and the cashier would just stare at him with this look of total disbelief.

Obviously, his ease with numbers would serve Ed well as an adult in both his day job as an electrician as well as kingpin of the policy racket in his sprawling auto plant. In his youth, however, he struggled to figure out how best to use his gift.

Despite an impressive academic record, Dad still considered himself something of a slacker. He could focus on work because that's how he made money. But when it came to the classroom, he could maintain a B average in high school without breaking a sweat – so that was all he did. Deep down, young Ed knew he could have done even better had he applied himself for report cards the way he did for paychecks.

As a youth, I was never told that if you get good grades, good things can happen, like scholarships, et cetera.

Here he was, this unmistakably brainy, gifted young black teen, but because he was black in the South of the 1940s with little or no guidance regarding the value of education, he didn't fully realize how much potential he had or how much he could achieve. He had experienced a fleeting taste of it in Detroit only to be thrust back into rural Georgia.

Dad told me on more than one occasion that he kept a B average because it was easy and he knew Hattie wouldn't yell at him. But if someone had explained to him all that he could be, had he really understood, he's certain he could have gotten all A's. But that was the problem: Nobody was telling him what he could become. At least, nobody in Roswell.

Had my grandmother and Samuel been wealthier or more connected, Ed almost certainly would have gone on to college. He might well have wound up at Morehouse or Howard or one of the other black colleges and universities in the South. He might have gone on to be a professor or an engineer or a mathematician.

But for all his mother and stepfather's efforts, the family couldn't afford to send Ed to college. So instead, after high school graduation, Ed took a job at a Roswell appliance store. He cleaned floors and shoved around heavy stoves and refrigerators all day, every day. He hated it. It was menial work, backbreaking and wholly dissatisfying even for a young man whose dreams weren't fully formed. The job paid enough to hold Ed for several months, but he grew more restless and unhappy with each passing season in Roswell.

That's when Ed Martin realized he wasn't a kid anymore. The relatively happy youth he enjoyed had morphed into an early adulthood marked by pushing freezers, bleak employment prospects, and a sharpening recognition of the limits Roswell's oppressive racial climate would place on his future. Jim Crow's daily slights – the legalized insults against black humanity and citizenship that marked life in Roswell since Ed could remember – were becoming too much. The pang of injustice he felt at not being able to attend his local high school had metastasized, first into simmering anger, then into an iron-clad determination to get out of Roswell forever.

But how to do it? Dad harbored only the haziest notions of professional success. With college out of the question, he wasn't quite sure what options were open to him. In some respects, though, that didn't matter much.

Displaying the practical side of his mother's nature even as a young man, Ed was far less concerned with how he made money than about the dreams money would allow him to fulfill. As long as he could work a good-paying job, any good-paying job, he would figure out how to make the rest happen. His earliest ventures outside of Roswell – his Detroit sojourn, the four-year shuttles to and from his Atlanta high school – clearly showed him there was a better life to be had in the big city.

He wanted to taste the best life had to offer, both literally and figuratively. While Ed often dreamed of fancy cars, shiny watches, and fine clothes, perhaps his greatest passion was for food. His years with his stepfather chef had given Ed Martin a surprisingly discriminating palate. Years after his death, friends would fondly recall Ed's love of fine pastries, entreés with unpronounceable names, and fancy restaurants he would travel hundreds of miles to visit.

He had grown up spending long hours after school and summers toiling alongside his stepdad in the kitchens of some of Roswell's nicer restaurants, sampling some of the best food the local upper crust could buy. Ed longed for the day he could sit as a customer inside the same sort of fancy bistros and high-end steakhouses whose patrons he serviced.

He also knew those desires would never be fulfilled in Roswell.

You couldn't drink out of a white water fountain. If we took the bus, we had to ride on the back seat of the bus. If the back got filled up, then we had to stand.

When I went to see that movie, Sounder, *I saw a lot of things that reminded me of back home.*

We had two restaurants, one that served all blacks, and one downtown that served all whites. I worked at both of them. There were only two or three of us in my stepfather's restaurant. He'd hire a white lady to work out front. It was the South back in the '40s and '50s. I worked there from 13 to 16 because at 17 I was working in the appliance store. I couldn't get ahead, not there. So I did what I had to do.

I ended up leaving and coming up to Detroit.

Detroit was the logical choice for Ed for a number of reasons. His father still lived there, as did some of the maternal relatives he'd stayed with in Hamtramck years before. Continuing to enjoy its reputation as the Arsenal of Democracy gained during World War II, Detroit was flush with jobs in the early '50s, thanks to a booming industrial sector built on the back of the city's auto industry. Ed knew there was good work to be had there.

Just as important, in northern cities like Detroit, social mobility among African-Americans didn't come with the same oppressive restrictions that were matter-of-course in the 1950s South. In Detroit, blacks owned gorgeous brick homes, ran successful businesses, and had carved out a vibrant cultural scene set to the sweet rhythms of blues and jazz. As a result, although segregation and racism were rampant in the Motor City, too, it was nevertheless becoming something of a mecca for many blacks. As Eddie put it:

My mother said I'd have a better chance if I came up here.

Hattie Stafford always wanted what was best for her children, and she knew the promise industrial cities like Detroit held for blacks from the South. Ed, who still warmly remembered his time with his Aunt Mattie in Hamtramck, knew there were just as many good times to be had as there was money to afford them. Time would prove them both right.

For much of Ed's adult life, Detroit turned out to be the haven he always had envisioned. Save for his military service overseas, Ed would call Detroit home for the rest of his life.

CHAPTER FOUR

Pickup Games

Back in Detroit, his once-and-future home, Dad spent a few months with his Aunt Mattie, the same relative who had welcomed him years earlier in Hamtramck. But it was not long until he moved again, this time into the home of his biological father, Charles. Dad had kept in touch with Charles but hadn't lived with him since infancy, until he settled into a small room of his house on Philadelphia Avenue.

Dad connected with a cousin about his age, Adolphus Porter, who set about reacquainting Ed with his city of choice. Ed Martin's life in Detroit was about to begin in earnest.

His father's house was in the North End, a bustling neighborhood of the northern edge's vital business and entertainment district. Together, the renowned Paradise Valley and Black Bottom were the pulsating heart of Detroit's black community.

When Ed arrived in Detroit in 1952, the North End was still vibrant and Paradise Valley was still the hub for black nightlife. Its allure was powerful enough to captivate a mischievous, wide-eyed 18-year-old from the South who was hungry for both fun and opportunity.

It didn't take long for Dad to throw himself into the street culture around Hastings Street, the major artery of African-American commerce. Dad spent more than a few hours inside the less respectable establishments along the thoroughfare. There, as was the case with almost everything Ed enjoyed, he couldn't just dabble in gambling. In typical fashion, he went full-bore.

Over the next few years, he became a student of the hustle, and the North End was his classroom. He honed his pool-shooting skills. He learned what it took to win at high-stakes card games. And he proved to be a quick study in the art of shooting craps. During this time, the ambitious country boy evolved into one of the most formidable gamblers in the city.

I'm pretty sure Dad learned to shoot pool while he was still in the South, but when he got up to Detroit he took it to another level and so we always had pool tables in our house. He lost the use of one eye when a lawn mower threw a shard of glass into his eye, but even that didn't seem to affect his game. He would still have all these young basketball players over at his house and be schooling them on the green felt, shooting what hustlers call "jack-up" pool, playing with only one hand.

Hastings Street also introduced Eddie Martin to what was at the time the most lucrative game of chance available in black communities: the street lottery, also known as the numbers game.

In the street lottery, bettors attempt to predict which three-digit number will be randomly selected the next day. (The winning number was determined by the total dollar amount of bets placed at racetracks the day before, a figure printed in newspapers the following day.) Bets flowed to the tune of tens of thousands of dollars each day. For all the money to be earned on the felt, at the card tables, and in backroom dice games, no hustle could match the numbers game.

Dad said the numbers were just a part of life in the neighborhood back then. You knew the dudes who shot dice, the ones who played cards, the guys who ran the numbers. Eddie wasn't deep into the game back then, though. He was observing – and learning.

He played the street lottery on occasion, and sometimes even took small bets from customers on behalf of the major numbers houses. He was little more than a rookie then, however, years away from becoming a master of the game.

For whatever time he spent hanging out on Hastings Street, Dad couldn't forget the hopes his mother had expressed for him when she urged him to move to Detroit. The goal of earning a good living was never far from his mind. While gambling was fun, Dad was determined to land one of those well-paying jobs that people had been flocking to Detroit for decades to find.

Ed worked a couple of odd jobs around town before landing his first steady gig with the health-care coverage provider Blue Cross. He spent more than a year as a clerk, filing and logging billing information, contract numbers, and other data for the insurance giant.

Dad always said he enjoyed his first-ever "real" job. The coworkers and supervisors were decent to him, and the hours were far kinder than what he'd known down South. It was a far cry from sweeping up store floors and shoving Frigidaires. But the pay was paltry, and for Ed, that made all the difference.

Even though he was barely an adult, he felt as if he had already worked a lifetime in low-paying jobs. He never shied away from hard work, but he was sick of doing it for pennies.

He calculated that he needed to make at least twice as much as he was earning at Blue Cross in order to remain in Detroit. He didn't want to leave the company, but cousin Adolphus was working at Ford Motor Company and kept whispering in his ear. "Man," he would say, "you could be doing so much better if you could get into the electrician apprentice program at Ford."

Finally, he took the drive to neighboring Dearborn, applied for an apprenticeship and, to the surprise of practically everyone except himself, passed the entrance exam with flying colors. Just like that, his weekly salary nearly doubled to almost ninety dollars. The only drawback was that Dad would have to go back to school, to Ford's apprenticeship program at Henry Ford Community College, as it is known today.

Despite Ford's diverse labor force and unconventional hiring practices, many jobs – especially in skilled trades – still were considered off limits to blacks.

The unions were rife with racism, and members often went to extraordinary lengths to keep African-Americans out of their ranks. Blacks who defied the odds and gained entrance into apprenticeship programs were confronted with bigoted instructors, double standards and hateful classmates who refused to study with them or share notes. For a black man, becoming an electrician at Ford in the 1950s was no stroll along the production line.

"The white guys would tell you to your face they weren't going to show you anything," Daniel Maynard told me. Maynard was a retired electrician who entered the Ford apprenticeship program years after Ed and worked with him in the '60s and '70s. "If you were black, they were trying to mess you up however they could. Even if you passed the test, if they knew you were black, they would just pass you over.

"Eddie had gone through the program before me, so if this was the case when I got in there, I know it had to be as bad or worse for him. But Eddie was sharp, too. He had to be. If you were a black electrician at that time, you were better than the white guys. Not because you were black, but because you had to be better just to get the job."

Given his Southern origins, Ed was used to confronting Jim Crow-like racial barriers. And he was used to getting around them. He knew that once he set his mind on a goal – whether it was landing a job, learning a skill or mastering a trade – he could practically will himself to accomplish it. All he had to do was focus.

The apprenticeship program would not prove much different. Over the next several months, Ed excelled in the classroom, even as he put in eight-hour shifts six days a week at the Ford Rouge Plant. Focus. Focus. That was the key, he said.

He finished the program in three years, posting an average grade of 96 out of 100. Upon graduation, he was promised an electrician's job at Ford. But first, he had another commitment to fulfill: Military service.

Ed had received a draft deferment from the Army while he finished his electrician's training, but once it was completed he knew he would be drafted so instead he volunteered to avoid getting stuck in the infantry.

Dad did his basic training at Fort Knox, Kentucky. He became a favorite with his fellow soldiers, he told me, in large part to his culinary skills. He was a hit in the mess hall, but if all he wanted was to sling hash, he could have stayed in Georgia and toiled in the restaurants around Roswell. He had bigger plans.

He told his superior officers that he wanted to pursue training in computers and missile systems. They approved his request, and after a short leave, he reported to a missile-training base in Oklahoma. But before basic training began, he felt something akin to the thrill of rockets being launched.

While he was on leave in Detroit before heading for Oklahoma, Ed Martin met someone.

It started as a blind date, and I'll bet that Hilda Baker didn't want to go. But a friend of hers kept urging her to meet some guy named Ed who worked at Ford and seemed really nice, so she finally, reluctantly, agreed.

Hilda quickly became more

Two major life changes came quickly for Ed Martin, his enlistment into the military, followed soon by his marriage to the poised and elegant Hilda Baker

than just another date. Short, thin, always well dressed and her long hair perfectly coiffed, she embodied a type of big-city class that instantly mesmerized Ed. She was keen on matters of etiquette and conduct. She was elegant.

In stark contrast to Ed's younger days, Hilda's upbringing had been solidly middle class. Her father earned a good living buying and renting real estate in Detroit's burgeoning black communities. She and her sisters graduated from Detroit's predominantly white Chadsey High School. The Bakers were bedrock members of what was then Zion Congregational Church of God in Christ.

But Hilda also knew how to have a good time and how to take the charming country transplant just as she found him. Consequently, she quickly took the place of pool hustling and poker games among Ed's preferred pastimes. They discovered a shared interest in good music and nights on the town. They went rollerskating. They slipped away to romantic lunches and movie dates.

And Hilda was just as taken with the charming, generous Mr. Martin as he was with her. "Oh, I was hearing about Ed even before I met him," recalls Lil Herndon, one of my Mom's four older sisters. "She was just overwhelmed by him, exceptionally delighted. I just remember thinking, 'Oh, I have to meet this young man.' And honestly, when I did, I felt the same way about Ed. He was special. He loved people. He loved family. He loved everybody. And that just really struck me. You don't meet people who like everybody, you know. They may say they do, but you have to prove it. And he did that. Oh, yeah, he was special."

The youngest of five girls, Hilda had been doted on by her father most of her life. She wasn't just used to attention: she reveled in it. "By her being the youngest, she was always a diva growing up," Herndon recalls. And in Eddie Martin, she had found a man who would be devoted to her for life.

On June 20, 1958, Ed married Hilda while he was home on leave. She joined him in Germany not long after. They toured Europe together, at times turning Ed's military stint into something more closely resembling a whirlwind honeymoon. They frequented clothing stores, restaurants, cultural attractions and nightclubs.

"They loved it," Lil Herndon said. "Hilda was a gourmet cook, and I remember her telling me how she had learned to cook German food. She was very excited about that. She told me about Switzerland, and the highways in Europe where you could drive as fast as you wanted. It was all fascinating to her. And she never got tired of it. She never got homesick. She was with Ed, so that meant she was having a great time."

After they returned to America, Ed abdicated all cooking duties to Hilda even though he himself was no slouch in the kitchen. In my entire life, I can remember only one time that he initiated a meal. He prepared a big kettle of chili, which he reheated and embellished for several days in a row. One unforgettable result of that venture was that it made me all the more appreciative of Mom's cooking.

Ed was discharged from the Army in 1959. After he and his bride returned to Detroit, he took the job Ford had promised him before he left, landing as an electrician in the automaker's sprawling Dearborn Engine plant. He and Hilda bought a house on the Detroit's east side.

Three years later, in 1962, my brother, Bruce was born. I came along fifteen months later.

Ed Martin had been gone from the South barely ten years. Yet he had journeyed a long, long way from Roswell.

In fact, his life was moving along nicely. Now a military veteran who had seen the world and become a skilled tradesman, he had a growing family, a new job he was settling into comfortably, and was earning three dollars an hour. With that kind of paycheck, Ed finally could enjoy the sort of lifestyle he only dreamed about when he first set off for Detroit.

Much as he enjoyed his brief stint at Blue Cross years earlier,

Ed said he couldn't have scripted a better workplace than the one provided by Ford.

"It wasn't a hard job. I worked 'til 6, 7 or 8 in the evening. I made money, raised a family. The plant was a good place to be. We played softball together. I'd gamble some. We had card games out there and I was pretty good.

"And I would sneak out. We had two or three people on the same job so we didn't all have to be there at the same time. One guy would be gone most of the time, then be back working before his shift ended. Sometimes we'd go out to the club. Every night at least one guy had a night out. I would get a couple nights a week. I'd come back to the job, of course. We always did that. But it was back and forth."

When he was actually working, Ed spent his days roaming the vast Dearborn Engine complex in search of minor problems – sputtering machines, erratic conveyer belts, faulty wiring. Rarely did he run across an issue he couldn't fix in a few hours.

The roaming nature of the job brought Ed into contact with workers from throughout the iron-and-concrete labyrinth of the Dearborn complex. From supervisors to assembly-line workers to the janitors and security guards, Ed got to know nearly everyone at the plant. And as had been the case for most of his life, most of them liked him.

Popular, good at his job and well compensated, Ed easily could have lived out the same unremarkable, blue-collar existence that defined thousands of his peers at the plant. But Ed Martin wasn't one to sit contentedly. He always seemed to want more: more to do, more to see, more to eat, more to spend. His job, challenging and technical as it was, still bored him. Doing it every day was the equivalent of shooting pool with both hands.

In the subculture of Detroit's auto factories, there was always much more going on than mere shift work. Indeed, the plants functioned less like industrial workspaces and more like small town, complete with their own neighborhoods, entrepreneurs and bustling economies. Just about anything that was available on the streets could also be obtained inside the plants: gourmet food, fine clothes, fancy cars, loans, drugs, gambling, even sex.

The car caverns could be dens of iniquity just as enticing as any of the Paradise Valley storefronts where Ed grew into manhood. Although Ford paid good wages, an enterprising worker could earn twice as much dabbling in the underground economy that thrived inside the sprawling complex.

And Ed Martin was nothing if not enterprising.

Since returning from the Army, he had become increasingly obsessive about gambling. In addition to the card games and pool hustles, Ed had started betting the horses. He became a shrewd handicapper, immersing himself for hours in newspapers and journals and racetrack forms in an attempt to pinpoint the day's best odds.

At the plant, he began learning more about the street lottery. He started off just placing a few bets for himself, hoping for a three-digit stroke of luck to bolster his paycheck a bit. That brought Ed into contact with the plant's "numbers runners," the people responsible for taking the bets and delivering them up the food chain to the numbers "houses" outside the plant. The houses, also known as "banks," were responsible for paying off any winners.

Ed, ever the analyst, began spotting flaws and inefficiencies among the runners working the Dearborn plant. Many of them moved so slowly around the plant, or were so restricted in their movements, that they couldn't get to all of the bettors who wanted to play. They would leave hundreds, sometimes thousands of dollars in potential bets unplaced.

Some runners weren't exactly math wizards and either got cheated or cheated the customers. Others had strict rules against accepting certain three-digit combinations, fearing that those bets, known as "cut numbers," were played too often. Ed, however, had none of these deficiencies.

As an electrician, his job took him into every corner of the plant and brought him in contact with almost every segment of the Ford workforce. He was free to go wherever and whenever he pleased. He was easy to get along with and hard not to like. Occasionally, he'd gather a throng of coworkers around him and present a variation on his supermarket checkout-line stunt.

"Give me a number at random! Anybody!" Ed requested.

"Five fifty!" someone might shout.

"Two twenty-three!" another might cry out.

"Seven Seventy-five!"

"Six twenty!"

He would listen quietly as several others rattled off figures, his eyes roaming the crowd, mind quietly churning. The moment the shouting stopped, Ed would calmly announce the sum of all the numbers thrown at him. And he was never wrong.

It became a show, entertainment for the workforce. It was sort of Ford's follies. And every time, workers would stand there amazed and someone would holler, "No way! That ain't right! That can't possibly be right! We gon' do that again!"

A couple guys would write the numbers down by hand. Somebody would pull out a calculator. They would nod their heads or go thumbs-up. And then Ed would ask them to call out numbers again. Every time, Ed would deliver the total. Correctly. The audience would be amazed.

Ed Martin had been at Ford less than two years and was about to take the numbers game to a new height.

For as long as anyone could remember, workers at the Ford plant had been playing the numbers. On top of that foundation, Ed knew he could attract new customers, knew he could "Do it better."

To get started, he hooked up with an old friend, a successful North End numbers man nicknamed Chop-Chop. We never knew Chop-Chop's real name. I'm not sure if even Ed knew it, because he tended to keep the streets separate from his family life. I do remember Chop-Chop as a hustler who already had been in the game for years, having started as a runner before moving up the ladder.

He was among a handful of mentors who had schooled a young Ed Martin when he first arrived in Detroit, teaching him the ins and outs of Paradise Valley nightlife. When Dad explained that he wanted to start running numbers out of the plant, he and Chop-Chop struck a deal in which Ed would gather those bets and turn them over to him. In return, Ed would receive a cut. He started with a nickel for every dollar turned in and, as he proved himself capable, his share rose to 25 cents. Should a plant worker hit the number, Chop-Chop would give Ed the money to take to Ford and pay the winner.

Gradually, as a way to better acquaint himself with the business, Ed began taking on some of the very small bets himself, turning in only wagers of a quarter or more to Chop-Chop, his "bank" on the North End.

The partnership worked smoothly for more than a year. Each workday, Ed would make his normal rounds at the plant, inspecting equipment and troubleshooting problems while he rounded up betting slips and the accompanying cash from Ford workers. The three-digit numbers usually were scrawled on small scraps of paper. Frequently, bettors were extended credit and allowed to settle their accounts on payday. He would collect his payments then run the slips and money to Chop-Chop's place and wait for that day's results.

One frosty winter afternoon, however, everything changed.

Ed had dutifully collected his numbers to give to Chop-Chop, but he was unable to find his friend. Several phone calls went unanswered. Finally Ed got the news from a mutual friend: His "bank" had gone out to shovel snow earlier that day and suffered a massive heart attack.

Chop-Chop was dead.

Even as Ed Martin mourned, he fretted about what to do next. He was responsible for securing bets at the Dearborn plant, but Chop-Chop always had been the "house," the one who underwrote each bet. Now Ed was holding a clutch of fresh bets with no house to cover them.

Ed could have taken the bets and gone looking for another house. The three-digit number would be out soon. If he was holding any winning bets, those customers would expect to be paid off by day's end.

Or, he simply could have walked away. Since he was only a runner, he technically wasn't responsible for paying off any winners. Tomorrow he could just go to work, explain that the "house" had keeled over and died, and leave his bettors to find someone else to handle their three-digit dreams.

Or maybe there was another option.

That night, Ed fell to his knees by his bedside. He began slowly pulling the scraps of paper from his pocket and turning over each one. Viewed separately, they didn't seem like much: A $1 wager here, a 50-cent bet there. Taken together, however, those tiny bits of paper could add up to hundreds, even thousands of dollars. And bets came in like this 'round the clock, shift to shift.

Sure, there was an occasional winner, but Ed knew the odds. Over time, the house wins.

So why not become the house? Why not take on all the action himself?

Yes, there would be considerable risk, at least early on. If several bettors had a consecutive string of winning numbers, Ed could be on the hook for tens of thousands of dollars, maybe more. Without Chop-Chop or another financier to back him, he could be broke and out of business before he ever got started.

However, if he could avoid booking any winning numbers – at

least for a few weeks until he accumulated enough cash – Ed could use the wagers to underwrite his own operation.

Still on his knees, Ed shoveled the last bits of paper under his bed. He muttered a brief prayer. Moments later, he stood up, resolute.

In that instant, Big Money Ed Martin was born. He was now the numbers man.

The next day, he went about business as usual, as if nothing had changed. But all the while, his mind was working, telling him one simple truth: if you don't have to turn money over to anyone, you get to keep it all.

It was the beginning of an ascent that, over the next 30 years, would see Ed Martin transform himself from talented skilled tradesman into one of the most infamous "boosters" in the history of college sports.

CHAPTER FIVE

Running Up the Numbers

When Ed Martin enlisted in the numbers game in the 1960s, he stepped into a domain entrenched in urban America since the turn of the century. He entered the world of the "policy kings."

Originating in European immigrant communities in the late 1800s, policy games had taken root in black communities throughout the North by the early 1910s. That was when the Great Migration began ferrying millions of blacks from farms and fields to flats and factories. By the 1920s, the games were part of a way of life for millions in the nation's swelling ghettos. Unlike 'ruinous' vices such as drugs and alcohol, the street lottery was viewed mostly benignly – respected even – by almost all but the straight-laced. For most, playing the numbers was no more harmful than a church bingo game. Some dabbled, others were obsessed. From the 1920s to the 1970s, it often seemed that nearly everyone in urban black America played the numbers or knew someone who did.

There were various systems for determining winners, and, although terms like "policy" and "the numbers" are now used interchangeably, these systems were once used to distinguish between the two. In the old-school policy games that had arrived with Italian immigrants in the 1900s, operators would drop several numbers into a giant drum and pull the winning numbers themselves. The enterprise was dubbed "policy," it is said, because bettors often made these wagers as insurance against other bets.

The numbers game, however, was said to have originated in the West Indies. Winning numbers weren't drawn by the banks, but rather were set according to random figures printed in the following day's newspapers. Winning numbers were often drawn from horse-race results that were printed in the paper. While systems varied, one common practice was to set the winning number by the final dollar digit of the day's total take for the first-, second- and third-place finishers.

Thus, if the day's first-place winners earned a total $1,127, second place $641 and third place $338, then the winning number would be 718. Eventually, this system, based on the pari-mutuel betting handle, became the most popular source for determining numbers, but it wasn't the only one. Some banks used combinations from the New York Stock Exchange as well as receipts from the US Customs House. These figures were also printed in local papers.

Because of their overwhelming popularity, numbers games exploded into some of the most lucrative businesses in black America. In his book *Kings, The True Story of Chicago's Policy Kings and Numbers Racketeers: An Informal History*, author Nathan Thompson estimates that, in African-American communities alone, policy games generated as much as $100 million a year during the 1930s.

In addition to the profits, the numbers rackets also provided employment for hundreds of thousands of blacks. Further, the numbers men often poured their illegal profits into an amazing variety of legitimate businesses, from convenience stores to hotels to newspapers to Negro Leagues baseball teams to barber shops to nightclubs and the building of churches.

The job opportunities that resulted were legion. They bankrolled political campaigns and even had a hand in underwriting social struggles like the early incarnations of the labor and civil-rights movements. It is no exaggeration to say that, during the first half of the 20th Century, the street lottery was an indispensable cog in the economic engine of black America.

The stage couldn't have been better set for Ed's ascent. In time, on the same shop floor where Henry Ford had built his empire, Ed Martin would carve out a realm of his own.

Building the Business

Ed limited his operation almost exclusively to the plant, a practice he maintained for the duration of his enterprise. His experience in the city had taught Ed to see "street business," the clientele outside the plant, as volatile and less reliable. He preferred the steady action that his gainfully employed co-workers predictably provided day in and day out.

Ed explained his first 60 days as the house this way:

Every day, I saved. I think I went 20 days without a hit. I might have had to pay out a nickel bet, but nothing high, no dollar bets. After that, I think I went another 20 to 30 days with no hits. So I built that money up. Now I had several thousand dollars. And I just kept going.

Still, receiving all of the profits wasn't necessarily the same as making a lot of money – at least not at first. As an unestablished "bank," Ed would have to out-hustle the better-known numbers operators who had been flourishing in the plant for decades. So, he moved slowly, adding only as many clients as he knew his small but growing bankroll could handle.

For the first six months, he ran his operation all by himself, gathering the betting slips, recording them in his book and, of course, paying out winnings. He couldn't just start recruiting people to turn in numbers to him. Not if he was going to pay the hits, too. And of course he had to pay. You don't stay in the numbers business very long if people think you're going to cheat them when they win.

Some operators held winnings for days before paying off the lucky bettor. Not Ed. He became known for paying up quickly, even the day of the bet if he was able to reach the winner. For his co-workers – many of whom lived paycheck to paycheck despite ample salaries – those payouts often helped them bridge the gap from one payday to the next.

Ed also earned favor in the plant for his willingness to book bets on what is known in the policy business as "cut numbers," numbers such as "123" which are bet heavily because they are favored by many players. Many other banks, even the larger operators, tended to shy from cut numbers out of fear that a run on them could dent or even destroy their business. Not Ed, though. He took cut numbers same as any other, and continued to do it years later, even after the street lotteries added four-digit bets.

But even beyond accepting cut numbers and making fast payouts, the biggest contributor to Ed's success was his affable personality. Many of the larger numbers banks were faceless to the plant workers, represented only by the runners who picked up bets and dropped off winnings. Not so with Eddie Martin – he was a daily presence. Handsome and always in high spirits, his short hair and full beard always immaculately groomed, Ed worked the shop floor like a campaigning senator, glad-handing and smiling at each workstation where he'd stop to pick up his betting slips. He chatted up his clients about matters great and small, ate lunch with them, tipped out with them to bars and restaurants.

As the years rolled by, Ed's business went from a trickle to a steady stream of bets. His clientele grew from a handful of bettors in the late 1960s to hundreds, aptly handled by his growing host of runners, less than a decade later. His operation expanded. In some instances, Ed was able to outmaneuver his competition. Other times, he won through sheer attrition.

While he still wasn't clocking what the city's bigger banks grossed week in and week out, Ed was now a respected player in the numbers racket inside the Dearborn plant. Ford Motor Company still employed Ed as an electrical troubleshooter, while the nature of his job at its Dearborn plant let him spend as much time running numbers in the factory as he did tending to wires and fuses.

Just as Ed's business began to pick up steam, the Detroit numbers game was rocked by a most unlikely new competitor: the State of Michigan. In May 1972, Michigan voters approved a constitutional amendment that allowed for the creation of a legal state lottery. By 1973, the state had awarded its first million-dollar payout. Four years after that, the Daily 3 three-digit lottery was available through online terminals. By 1981, the state added a four-digit drawing as well. After more than a century of criminalizing the policy business – and, of course, the entrepreneurs who built it – in less than ten years, the state had heavily muscled in on the numbers racket. As a result, both a way of life and an entire underground economy that had thrived since the early 1900s were thrown into jeopardy.

While the illegal lottery was drying up for some by the late 1970s, Ed had managed to adapt to the new competition. Already known for paying out quickly, he made his payouts even faster – turning over winnings within hours of a hit sometimes – so as to beat the state. Where the state demanded a minimum $1 bet, Ed emphasized that he still allowed bettors to wager as little as a quarter. He extended credit to more players. Additionally, he was quick to remind his clients, that he paid $600 for every $1 straight 3-digit hit compared to the State's $500. All in all, he would point out to whomever would listen, the illegal lottery was still a better bet than the Michigan Lottery.

It's Time to Make a Black Man Rich

So, even as the state lottery grew in popularity, Ed managed to expand both his client list and his roster of workers. In fact, perhaps the single biggest boon to Ed's business came in 1982, about a decade after the creation of the state lottery. Impressed both with Ed's persistence and his business-like meticulousness, several veteran numbers runners in the Ford plant system began to defect from other banks to Ed's operation, bringing with them scores of fresh clients. That year, Ed's business inside the plant grew exponentially.

Two runners were particularly significant. One was a numbers operator named Jesse Keesee, a production-line worker for several years at Ford. Keesee had become known as one of the most prolific – and trustworthy – numbers runners on the shop floor. His client list included dozens of new gamblers, all dedicated to playing with him every day.

Another was Bennie Smith, a squat, gravelly-voiced man with thick hands and thicker glasses who was known both for his street smarts and his loyalty. Like Keesee, Smith had long ago made his name as a go-to man for Ford workers looking to place a few wagers. Additionally, Smith's good name had won him the confidence of multitudes of gambling auto workers.

For years, Keesee and Smith both turned in their business to a numbers operator nicknamed Cowboy. But as Cowboy's business grew, he turned the reins over to his daughter and she didn't run the business with the same humility, deference and attention to customer service as Cowboy. Her style and attitude chafed the gentlemen hustlers in her organization. When Ed approached some of the gents about joining his team, many were more than ready to make the switch.

"It wasn't a big deal or anything. He just came up to me one day and told me he wanted to talk to me about doing business with him," says the now-retired Keesee, "I knew who he was, of course. Everybody on the force back then knew Eddie Martin. He was a good guy, one of the most well-known guys in the plant as a matter of fact. He told me he could offer me 25 percent on the business that I brought in. That was good money because I knew I was taking a lot of bets. So I told him that I was interested."

Smith, meanwhile, says his first motivation was the money, too – but, as a throwback to a time when black numbers men dominated the street lottery in his old Black Bottom neighborhood, he relished the idea of a black man at the helm of a major numbers racket. Says Smith: "I didn't mind working for anybody, regardless of color. But I knew Ed and I liked him. He was always friendly and good people. I had spent years making a white man rich. So I decided, 'You know what, it's time to make a black man rich.'"

The new clients Keesee and Smith brought over, combined with the workers who were already playing with Ed, soon turned Ed into one of the most influential players in the city's numbers racket. Even as incursions by the state were eroding other players' bankrolls, Ed's hustle was growing ever stronger. He wasn't just treading water in the numbers game at the plant anymore. He was now running one of the most lucrative number operations in the entire city. His weekly gross betting volume was $50,000-80,000. At a 10-20% profit he was averaging $10,000 a week.

Some evenings I would go with my dad to the plant to learn how he managed the business so I could handle it when he was on vacation. Inside the plant, I would walk about fifty yards to a balcony. At this time of the evening the plant appeared strangely serene. The highly polished concrete floors gleamed even in the dim light. The only sound was a dim humming from standby power of idle machinery. In the air there was always a faint smell of lubricant.

From the balcony, I would walk to a locker room that had benches and showers for the workers to change after their shift. My dad had bent one of the small slots in his locker so players could slide a small bundle of number slips inside of it. I had the combination and I would pick up the four or five bundles inside.

I would leave the locker on the opposite side and walk the same balcony for about a hundred yards, overlooking long assembly lines that were not very active. There I could go down a set of stairs to the plant floor. Under the stairs was a large metal cage enclosed in heavy-duty wire mesh. It housed several tool boxes and other utilities for the tradesman in this part of the facility. Ed had three tool boxes, one of which kept the records for the number business. I would pull out the records, retrace my steps out to the parking lot, and head home. There I would add everything up and see if anyone hit that night.

When I went with Dad, he would wear his safety glasses and that little paper hat. It made me chuckle that there were bikes available for him to ride around inside the massive plant. It made sense, but I always found it slightly humorous that my 60-year-old father rode bikes at work.

During a typical trip to the plant, a few workers would show up to play a last-minute number or two. Dad would gladly accept them. He also liked to work the business while he was there in the evening, all the while adding up in his head all the slips as he got them, never using a calculator or even a pen, never making a mistake.

One important item of equipment was a small television set kept secured in the cage. We had to play around with the antenna so we could hear the Ohio number because he took bets on the Detroit and Ohio numbers. If someone hit, we would go right out onto the floor and pay the winner. The winning number was also posted in the lunch room and people would come in, check it out and you could predict you would hear the groan when they saw they didn't hit.

From 1991 to 1999, every Friday Ed would carry around about $20,000. That was his stash for cashing the company checks of the people who owed him money for plays they made during the week. He had singles, fives, tens, twenties, fifties and hundreds in bulk as well as change to balance everyone to the penny. Even though several people knew he carried such cash, not once did anyone attempt to rob him.

Ed took the checks he needed to cash to Manufacturers Bank on Seven Mile Road and Maine. It was a large bank with a big lobby and two business windows. Soon after he started frequenting the bank, everyone in the branch knew him. Before long, he knew all of their birthdays, from the bank manager to each teller. He brought in perfume and other gifts throughout the year. He created such good will at the bank that as soon as he walked in the door, they called him up to the window to cash his checks. Sometimes he would call ahead to let them know the total and they would have his cash waiting for him when he arrived.

Hustling with Honor

As business grew, so did the profits. By the 1980s, Ed's lottery business was paying him as much as *five times more* than what he was earning at Ford.

Ed's lifestyle evolved along with the success of the business. He went from the inexpensive sports cars he owned while he was in the military to a succession of Mercedes-Benz sedans. He developed a taste for glitzy watches. His closets were packed with designer suits, fancy coats and jackets, expensive branded sweat suits, ostrich-skin boots and alligator-skin dress shoes, tailored shirts and overpriced sneakers.

And then there were the restaurants.

An ardent foodie since he spent his youth working with his stepfather in the fancy restaurant kitchens around Roswell, Georgia, satisfying his appetite went from indulgence to a mandate. I remember watching him pore over food sections of newspapers for articles on new restaurants, great chefs and unique meals. All it took was one good review and Dad would load the family into the car and we'd be off for a new dinner spot.

One time, Dad read a review of five-star restaurant named

The Wellington in Arlington Heights, Illinois. Within a week, he loaded up Hilda, his niece, Marsha Lynn and her partner, Frank, and flew them all there for the dining experience. There wasn't one four- or five-star restaurant within a hundred miles of our house that we didn't visit, including Jacques Petit Jardin, The Van Dyke Place, and The Lark.

Ed Martin didn't just patronize upscale restaurants — he breathed his own brand of life into them. He struck up conversations with everybody. He had to talk to the waiter and the maître'd. He would go on and on about a meal — he just had to meet the person who prepared this delicious dish. Often the chef would be summoned to our table for a personal thank you and a chat.

Somehow, even as life changed abruptly around him, Ed managed to remain generous and affable. He didn't wear his wealth as a badge of superiority. And almost anyone who'd known him had, in ways big or small, been touched by his generosity. For all his success, it seemed that few people begrudged him his nice homes or fancy cars or expensive boots or wads of big bills. He could grab your attention with a flashy ride or four-figure coat in one instant and in the next — with an avuncular smile and a few jokes — make you look past his extravagance.

My father's material desires weren't driven by any need to diminish others, but rather by the same aesthetic appreciation of quality that would draw him to the basketball players he would embrace years later. Skill and craftsmanship were supreme to him.

To Ed Martin, the proof was in the performance, whether that manifested itself in the effortless synchronicity of high-end watches, the sexy growl of European luxury cars, the culinary brilliance of a master chef or the sight of an All-America power forward thundering to the hoop. In fact, it may surprise you to learn that one of his favorite vehicles was the Volkswagen Beetle. He owned three of them over his lifetime as I recall, one blue, one beige, one red. Why? Performance.

He admired the simplicity and precision of the car's German engineering, the fact that it could run all day on a gallon of gas, and best of all, its size. When he would take me to Detroit Lions football games as a youngster when the team played at old Tiger Stadium, parking around the ballpark was at a premium. Dad loved the fact that he could park his VW in the tiniest spaces close to the field and walk away without caring about damage. It was his utility vehicle! But in 1980, when the first Ford Escorts were available in the U.S., the Ford employee took advantage of his discounts and switched to the brand-new compact.

There was a curiosity that drove much of his spending, a desire not just to buy things, but to examine them up close, to educate himself about them so as to more fully appreciate their distinguishing qualities. Ed liked nice things because, well, they were nice.

Perhaps it was a way to make up for what he felt he missed out on as a younger man, for opportunities lost by not going to college or making better life choices. Still, he wanted to attain a certain lifestyle. Money from the plant is good, he acknowledged to himself, but there's more to life that more money can bring me. And that's what the numbers allowed him to do.

But it was not without costs.

As much as we were enjoying Ed's newfound success, my mom still harbored persistent and deep misgivings. Ed was making more money than either of them had ever seen, and she always worried that their comparative prosperity, coupled with Ed's generosity and sociability, made her husband a target. True, organized crime elements had tried to muscle in on some numbers banks. Even so, the numbers racket had never been especially violent and Ed operated discreetly, but nonetheless, Mom was fearful.

It wasn't just a hunch either. Mom had felt that blowback personally. In 1964, years before Dad had immersed himself in the street lottery, when he was still just a fixture at local card games and race tracks, there had been an incident. Thieves who knew he gambled heavily broke into our home on Shields Street on Detroit's Northeast side. Dad was working midnights at Ford back then and Mom was home alone when they broke in. They threatened her life, tied her up, and ransacked the house. She wasn't hurt, but when dad came home early the following morning and found his wife still bound, he was nearly hysterical with fear and rage.

He was as mad at himself as he was at anyone else. Weeks before, a cousin who'd gotten wind of the plot to rob our house had tried to warn him. But Dad had pretty much ignored the warning.

The robbery prompted some major changes. Shortly thereafter, the family moved about a mile away to Conant Gardens. Dad cut back on his own gambling, limiting the card games he had so long enjoyed, and grew more careful with whom he associated.

For a time, he would just go to work and come straight home. But only for a time. Gambling was in his blood. He needed another outlet for his passion. He found it at the horse track.

Ed's familiarity with the policy game had taught him the basics of horse racing as a sport. He knew about odds, handles and the pari-mutuel betting system. But he could never be satisfied with only rudimentary knowledge of a subject he cared about. And so, he threw himself fully into the science of horserace betting, taking long hours to pore over betting sheets, race journals and sports pages. He became a regular at tracks such as the Hazel Park Raceway, in suburban Detroit. Predictably, he developed his own betting system.

As former fellow Ford electrician Daniel Maynard recalled, "Ed would go to the track, and he'd only bet on one horse. He'd tell me, 'I make a bet. If the horse wins, I go home. If the horse loses, I go home.' Eddie wasn't your typical gambler. He did that to make money. See, most gamblers just want to play. I've seen guys win $15,000 and not quit... they want a ton of money. Eddie was disciplined in everything he did. That's why he was so well-off financially. He did things where he knew he'd make a lot of money in a hurry."

Mom was comforted by the purchase of a new home and Dad's switch from cards to the ponies. But her fears and suspicions never totally went away. Her husband was still too giving, she worried, still too trusting. And as long as he was making a killing running one of the most lucrative numbers operations in Detroit, she knew that her family would always be vulnerable.

So while she never badgered her husband, Hilda Martin was the one person who regularly urged him to keep a low profile and a small circle of friends. If she thought he was being ostentatious or naïve about a friend's motives, she told him. Even as everyone else around Ed reveled in the moment, his wife fretted over what the future might bring.

We didn't talk much about our business to others, but inside the family, there was definitely worry and my mother felt a foreshadowing of what might be just over the horizon.

Ed acknowledged those concerns and tried to allay them. He didn't do business with 'street' clientele, he'd remind her. He no longer gambled in seedy places. He went to work every day – unassuming as ever in his work boots, jeans and plaid shirts with the pocket protectors – and always made his way back home to his family. Sure, he had his obsessions, a jones for good food, nice clothes and fancy cars. And, yes, he liked making bets as much as he liked taking them.

Ed's exceptional charitableness insulated him from excessive envy among co-workers. More importantly, he cultivated an understated work persona. He was plain-spoken, dressed simply for work, and was unfailingly friendly. As well as he lived outside the plant, inside the walls of Dearborn Engine, Ed was in many ways still an unassuming Georgia transplant.

He was fair in his dealings with bettors. He never cheated anyone and, even though clients would occasionally try to put scams past Ed – claims that a runner had taken down the wrong bet were heard frequently enough – Ed was always known to resolve matters peacefully (albeit usually in his favor). Though husky and broad-shouldered, he projected affability and charity. Like the old-school numbers men who preceded him, Ed fancied himself a "gentleman hustler," his quiet little enterprise no more hurtful than your typical church bingo game.

To be sure, state and federal prohibitions placed his business firmly on the wrong side of the law. But after nearly a century of criminalizing the policy game, the great state of Michigan had suddenly transformed itself into the largest bank on the street. What made Ed any worse?

As Ed saw it, whatever distinctions existed were minimal and, largely, cosmetic. His enterprise might've been criminal in a strict sense, but he prided himself on hustling with a measure of honor. He profited not because he was slimy but because he was smart, so why shouldn't his business flourish? As long as his anonymity held, he reasoned, as long as the world at large saw Eddie Martin not as a policy king but as just one more workaday drone toiling away in industrial obscurity, everything would be fine.

CHAPTER SIX

The Hook

When he began attending Southwestern High School games, Ed Martin had no clue how that would dramatically change the future. He couldn't foresee that what he was watching would not only alter the balance of power for high-school basketball in the city and state, but also have an impact that would echo through the halls and courts of college programs and pro teams for many years to come.

It was just another example of fortuitous timing for Big Ed. That's the way it always was with my father. As much as he benefited from his smarts, his work ethic, and his deft managing of money, he also profited from a remarkable knack for being in the right place at the right time.

First, it was the sudden death of Chop-Chop that propelled him from the ranks of the numbers runners into the role of a numbers house operator. Then it was his chance proximity in his workplace to the father of Michigan's single best basketball talent. It seemed that Ed Martin walked with an angel on his shoulder, so it should have been no surprise that he would inadvertently wander into the beginnings of a basketball dynasty.

Ed wasn't just watching the emergence of a lone star in Antoine Joubert. He was bearing witness to a veritable constellation of stellar prep talent across metropolitan Detroit, a golden age that would produce some of the most skilled, prolific and iconic basketball talent ever to ascend to the college and professional ranks.

There were, for example, the dominant Detroit Northern High Eskimo teams led by the gifted, punishing Derrick Coleman in the mid-1980s. There were scrappy teams like the Detroit Cooley Cardinals and their immensely adept center (and future NBA cautionary tale) Roy Tarpley. There were the Pershing Doughboys and the unstoppable Steve Smith. There were flashy, improbably deep squads with nicknames like the "Supreme Court" of Detroit Kettering and the "Sixth Fleet" of Detroit Denby, which also produced NBA journeyman Viktor Alexander.

This abundance of talent didn't just percolate through the city proper in the Detroit PSL either. Suburbs such as Romulus saw celebrated players like Terry Mills and Grant Long emerge. The northern suburbs of Birmingham and Beverly Hills boasted B.J. Armstrong and Shane Battier. In the Catholic School League, Scott Nichols, Negele Knight and Willie Burton (eventually one of the few players to ever score 50 points in the NBA) were leading Detroit St. Martin DePorres to back-to-back state titles.

Meanwhile, in the Michigan cities of Flint, Saginaw and Grand Rapids, players like Mark Macon, Glen Rice, Loy Vaught and Andre Rison were spearheading squads that were every bit as good (and sometimes better) than the powerhouses that loomed over the Detroit Public School and Catholic School leagues.

But while there may have been better teams that sometimes boasted better players, no single program mined that golden age with greater team success than the high school that, fittingly, dubbed themselves the Prospectors.

As a 6-foot-5 guard at Detroit Southwestern in the early 1980s, Antoine Joubert wasn't merely a high-school superstar. To much of the Motor City's basketball cognoscenti, he was an icon even before he'd earned his diploma.

Nicknamed "The Judge" (in response to rival Kettering High's "Supreme Court" boast), he combined a smooth outside jumper,

FRONT ROW: Joseph Hines, Carlton King, Orlando Milton, Kwesi Troutman, Howard Eisby, Quincy Bowens, Marcus Wourman, and Terrance Watson. BACK ROW: Coach Watson, Voshon Leonard, Micheal Hamilton, Jalen Rose, Garland Mance, Elton Carter, Kenneth Riley, Byron Johnson, and Michael Lovelace.

The 1988-89 Southwestern High School team was runner-up in the state playoffs, featuring several players who went on to college fame

deceptive quickness and near-telekinetic dribbling prowess into a game that was virtually unstoppable at the high-school level. One of the state's most prolific scorers ever, Joubert is 12th all-time in career points among Michigan preps with 2,208. He is also one of only three players in the history of Michigan high-school basketball to twice score more than 800 points in a season. (Magic Johnson did it only once at Lansing Everett High.)

In addition, Joubert shares the state record for most points scored through the final three rounds of the Michigan prep-basketball tournament with 122. As a senior in 1983, he set what was then a record for the Michigan Class A championship finals, pouring in 47 points in Southwestern's heartbreaking loss to Flint Central. (He scored 44 points in an earlier tournament game.)

That same year, Antoine Joubert was named the best player in the state.

Joubert was the cornerstone of a Southwestern program that,

over the next decade, would evolve into one of the most dominant high-school basketball powers ever. The Judge came to personify the up-tempo, hard-nosed style of play that became Southwestern's hallmark and produced such a rich lineage of high-school All-Americans, collegiate champions and future pros.

Along the way, Antoine also became Ed Martin's gateway into the world of amateur athletics.

Joubert recalls meeting my dad in about 1981, during his sophomore year, through his father, Zeke Joubert Sr. The two men worked at Ford's Dearborn Engine plant, with Zeke pouring concrete and doing other masonry work around the installation. Both were steeped in plant culture, so Zeke was in the circles that Ed flitted in and out of. Ed said the two of them had become fast friends long before Antoine was even in high school. They were two blue-collar tradesmen bonding over shared toil as well as a taste for strong drink and games of chance.

Those ties are what eventually led Ed to go to a Southwestern game. "They were already good buddies before I ever met Ed," Antoine says. "Then I guess what happened was I had made the paper. I'd made it a few times my freshman year, but my sophomore year I was starting to get in the paper a lot. So, I guess he came to my dad and asked 'Is this your son?' And that is how it all started."

Antoine can't remember exactly what game he had just finished playing in when he first met Ed. He does recall that students, parents, teachers and fans were jumping up and down and shouting in a victory celebration. Amid the pandemonium inside the cramped gym, Antoine turned and saw his dad standing with another man who had sauntered out of the bleachers and staked out a spot near the team's bench. Ed extended his hand, congratulated young Joubert, and shouted over the din, "Great game! I'll be watching you."

In that moment, a relationship was struck that would flourish over the next several years and endure for a lifetime. It did not take long for Antoine Joubert to become the first in what would be a long line of "Ed's guys."

"Our relationship evolved pretty quickly after we met," Antoine says. "Carl and Bruce were close to my age. Our parents got along. We hung out together, did a lot of different things. We went out to eat. We'd go over to their house, shoot hoops in the driveway, talk, things like that. We became like a family."

From Horses to Hardwood

For the rest of Joubert's sophomore year, Southwestern High games became both a haven for Ed and his newest obsession, one that would soon exceed all others. Once in the gym, Zeke and Ed would take the spot in the bleachers that commanded the best view of the action. Typically, Ed would be decked out in expensive shoes with a fancy jacket or wearing one of his high-end sweat suits. Together, Zeke and Ed would cheer like mad. After the game, Ed would leave for a while to attend to the details of his daily number business. Afterwards he would meet up with Zeke again. Ed said he always paid for those good times with Zeke, enjoying good food, drinks and music at home and at local restaurants.

> *I bought all the food and the drinks at the parties. I more or less paid for everything because Zeke played the lottery with me... I never gave him and his wife no money. I just bought and paid for everything. I was there, the party was going on and I had the most money.*

That was a pattern that Ed would repeat years later with other athletes and their families. There would be countless outsized meals, endless rounds of birthday celebrations, and signing-day fetes and graduation parties. No one questioned Ed Martin's motives. Nobody doubted his sincerity. As for Ed, he basked in a third-hand reflection of young Joubert's burgeoning celebrity, regardless of whether he got anything else in return. For him, it was enough to be in the mix, to simply to be able to say he knew the prep star.

There was another factor – Ed had always simply loved sports. His growing passion for Southwestern was an extension of an interest in prep hoops since his own teen years. He was mesmerized by the purity of high-school games, the electricity of the crowd, the unbridled hustle of the players. He loved analyzing the intricacy of the schemes and the coaches' decisions as they sent in plays from the sidelines.

> *I had a particular interest in high-school sports starting at Booker T. Washington High School. I used to go to all the games in high school – girls and boys. When I moved to Detroit, I attended the City and State Championship games. I remember back in the '60s and '70s going to see guys like Reggie Harding and Magic Johnson play. By me working with Antoine's father, I really got hooked on it again. I'd say '80 and '81 were the two big years that I really got back into it heavy.*

But this time around was different. His bond with Antoine made Ed feel more vested in the games, more personally impacted by their outcomes. The games meant something to him now. He found himself rooting harder for Southwestern than he had for any school since his beloved Booker T. Washington in Atlanta. Night after night, he'd leave the games hoarse and on a high from the charged-up high-school crowds.

With each game, his interest intensified. Ed found himself undergoing an unexpected transformation. An inveterate gambler for much of his life, he realized one day that he was losing his taste for the ponies. Between his numbers business, his day job and his growing interest in Southwestern High varsity boys basketball, Ed barely had time anymore to scour the track reports and handicap his races. And he no longer cared. What had started as a night out at a high school basketball game with a co-worker had evolved into an obsession. Ed had fallen hard for Southwestern hoops, and like a love-struck teenager, he couldn't get enough of the object of his affection.

True to his nature, Ed was never going to be satisfied being just an ardent fan. He saw something special in this team that transcended even his support for Antoine. With something almost like desperation, he threw himself into it just as he had with the numbers business or food or his other near-obsessions.

It was a familiar scenario, this getting hooked on excellence, challenging himself to gain that deep and honest insight into how something great worked. The new object of his obsessive nature was that the Southwestern High basketball team riveted Ed Martin with team play and passion. Other than Antoine and maybe one or two other players, there were no future college stars, let alone NBA-caliber ballers. What set them apart from almost every other team in the state for a decade was simple – it was their work ethic, discipline and conditioning. For Dad, it was no different than enjoying a great meal, having a nice watch, or just appreciating a finely tuned car engine.

I knew when he would come home to tell me about it that this was something big for him. He would rave about Antoine, of course, but then go on and on about the coaching strategy and other aspects of the game.

Years later he told me it was that Southwestern basketball team that drew him away from the track. That in turn stimulated him to do other things with his time. He discovered that he wanted to do what he could to help those young men.

But first, Ed had to get access. He may have been close personal friends with the team's star, but he was a stranger to the program as a whole. A few other players knew only that he was a friend of the Jouberts. He needed a path to the rest of the team, and there was only one route into the heart of the Southwestern program – through the team's hard-nosed, streetwise head coach.

The "P. Watt" Connection

Perry Watson had taken the reins at Southwestern in 1979, the same year Antoine Joubert had enrolled. Having been raised in southwest Detroit, Watson knew well that the neighborhoods around the high school brimmed with athletic talent. That fact hadn't always translated into basketball success. Many of the best athletes in the surrounding neighborhoods either eschewed organized sports in favor of the streets or preferred baseball to hoops.

The kids quickly dubbed their new no-nonsense coach "P. Watt." Watson was himself a Southwestern grad. After serving as the junior-varsity coach and a varsity assistant, Watson took over as varsity head coach in 1979. He immediately installed a grueling conditioning program that daily tested the physical endurance and emotional fortitude of even his best athletes. Watson demanded that his players be able to apply full-court pressure for an entire game if need be – and to do so without sacrificing speed and crispness on offense. As one of the most fertile prep proving grounds in the nation, the Detroit Public School League featured teams that were arguably as talented and as deep as the Southwestern Prospectors. But Watson was determined that no team would ever outwork his squad.

The impact of Watson's regimen was quickly apparent. Led by junior Leslie Rockymore and the precocious freshman Joubert, the Prospectors ended a playoff drought for the school that had reached back to the 1960s. By the end of Joubert's sophomore season in 1981, Southwestern finished with an 18-4 record and won nine in a row culminating with the PSL Championship which included a win over the Cooley Cardinals who were led by Roy Tarpley. And even though Rockymore had earned a basketball scholarship to the University of Michigan, and would leave Joubert the team's lone unquestioned leader for the 1981-82 season, Watson's plan to reinvigorate Prospector basketball was going to pay heavy dividends for many years to come.

Meanwhile, even as Watson was methodically orchestrating the Prospectors' turnaround, Ed Martin was slowly wending his way into Watson's sights. By the early '80s, he had already become a regular at Southwestern games, but Watson hadn't noticed him. Then, one day in the spring of 1981, Ed went to watch a practice of the Southwestern baseball team. That team was also coached by Watson and featured Rockymore, Joubert and a few other two-sport stars.

As my father remembered it, Watson was cleaning up after his team, gathering bases, balls and bats as his players slowly made their way back into the school. As they filed inside, Watson looked up to notice that Rockymore wasn't among them. Instead, his star player was several feet away, leaning into the driver's side window of a shiny green Mercedes-Benz, talking to a man draped in a fancy leather coat. Even from a distance, Watson would have been able to tell that coat cost serious money. Watson could also conclude that whomever Rockymore was talking to in that car could not be from the neighborhood.

After a few minutes, Rockymore meandered into the building, followed by Watson. When the two of them reached the school gym, the coach asked his center about the man in the Benz.

As my father reconstructed it later, the conversation went something like this:

That's Ed Martin, Rockymore said with a casual shrug, as if the name alone should've sufficed for his coach. It didn't.

Watson, ever wary of the wrong type of people getting close to his players, kept probing: But who is he, Rock?

Rockymore responded, He's just a good guy. I kinda just met him.

Watson pressed: And what did he want?

Rockymore wasn't quite sure how to explain his chat

to Watson, paused a while and said, it was weird, coach.

He just came over and started talking to me about U of M.

More specifically, Ed Martin had given Rockymore some interesting news: When the star ballplayer arrived at the Ann Arbor campus, he wasn't going to be rooming with Eric Turner, the best high-school point guard in Michigan, and the player who led his team to the Class A State Championship. Instead, Rockymore was getting a different roommate. Rockymore hadn't heard anything about this, but somehow the bearded man in the Benz seemed to know more than he himself did. Weeks later, Rockymore got a call from the school confirming the very same switch that Ed had told him was coming.

Watson was intrigued briefly, curious about this flashy stranger who seemed to have some sort of insider tie to the Michigan program. Watson didn't tolerate distractions to his program and would have had Ed immediately barred from any of his practice fields had he suspected him of being a bad influence. Somehow, though, he wasn't alarmed. And after he didn't see Ed at the baseball practices anymore that season, Watson essentially forgot about the man who had a Benz the color of money.

By the time basketball season resumed that fall, Ed was long since hooked. He continued to go to every game along with Zeke. Becoming Watson's friend, however, was proving to be difficult enough, but having access to his players was obviously going to be many times tougher. For the entire 1981-82 regular season and PSL playoff run, Ed watched from the stands with Zeke.

Then came March Madness. Southwestern made it to the quarterfinals as an underdog in a big game. No one expected them to go to Benton Harbor in west Michigan and win.

History had proved that teams just didn't go to Benton Harbor and beat that squad in their home gym. Apparently, no one told Antoine that. He had one of those games. He scored 10 of his team's first 12 points, finishing up with 39 points and 16 rebounds and the Prospectors walked off the court with the win. Ed was starting to feel a part of the Southwestern movement. To celebrate the big victory, he wanted to treat everyone to a meal. He mentioned that to Zeke and Antoine and quickly the word spread to all the players, coaches and family members who had made the two-hour commute.

The buzz was that they were going to do something above McDonald's, perhaps go to Big Boy. Zeke was standing beside Coach Watson when someone tapped him on the shoulder. And, of course, it was Ed Martin. Ed politely introduced himself to Coach Watson and told him he was proud of what he and the team had accomplished. He proposed that the team, coaches and family members all go out together to Big Boy. Watson smiled and nodded a polite no thanks – he had only enough money to feed the players at McDonalds. To that Ed just grinned and told Coach Watson he could keep his money because this was on him.

Once inside the restaurant, Perry Watson – being a street-wise kid himself from southwest Detroit – was concerned that this Ed Martin fellow might walk out on the bill. So, he stationed his assistant coaches by the door to make sure this volunteer host wouldn't try to dine and dash. That was the first of countless after-game meals courtesy of Uncle Ed. It was his entre into the Southwestern High basketball program.

A few days later, Big Ed told P. Watt that whatever he and the team needed, he would make sure he got it. Then, after the next few games, Ed reminded Watson that he had his full support.

It's not clear whether Watson took Ed seriously at first, but it's highly unlikely. Watson hated distractions and was notoriously protective of his team. Even before the Prospectors program became a powerhouse, he didn't trust anyone who tried to get too close to his kids. Still, Ed was charming and persistent and didn't seem to be asking for anything in return. Plus, he was already close with the program's biggest star, Joubert, and that didn't seem particularly detrimental.

As usual, Ed wasn't taking no for an answer. It wasn't long after his first few meetings with Watson that Ed became a fixture at Southwestern games and practices. He would often pull into the parking lot outside the school and wait for players to come over for Gatorade, jugs of water, and snacks. Along with those treats, he dispensed pep talks, words of encouragement, and reminders that all he wanted was to help with whatever was needed.

Everything that came afterwards can be traced back to Ed Martin's first look at Antoine "The Judge" Joubert. Did this man who became notorious years later for supplying gifts and cash to college stars, ever shower Joubert with gifts? Even though other former Southwestern players have profusely praised Ed Martin for his charity to them and their families, the question has been asked countless times: How much of Ed's generosity fell on Southwestern's superstar, Antoine Joubert?

It is true that Joubert, a man who remains my friend to this day, was the very first of the stars to be showered with gifts from Big Ed. In a very literal sense, it was open-handed generosity when money would pass from Ed to Antoine or to another young player in one of his "cash handshakes." Or there would be gifts of cakes, clothes, shoes and sneakers. The generosity that Ed would eventually export to Ann Arbor was first directed at Joubert.

It started in small ways with Antoine and I remember how my father chuckled when he talked about buying things for him:

Antoine used to tell his dad that I'd always buy him a hamburger. But I bought him a suit once. And he drove my car when he played a high-school game at the Michigan State Fairgrounds once. I let him use it and I came over with somebody. If he got jammed and needed $20 or something here or there, I'd help, but it wasn't that often.

My father's generosity to the Jouberts went beyond even these gifts, though. He bought him shoes, clothes and even a big fur jacket that Joubert was often seen sporting around Detroit. Joubert would never see the sums that Ed would later spend on future Michigan players such as Chris Webber, Robert Traylor or Maurice Taylor. But few, if any, of those who were close to the Southwestern program in the 1980s and early '90s deny that Ed's influence and charity touched every single coach and player in the program at some point or another. And that most certainly includes Antoine "The Judge" Joubert, the cornerstone star of the dynasty that Watson would build.

From the very beginning, however, Big Ed's generosity wasn't limited to the superstars.

Johnny Johnson, a rotund guard who played alongside Joubert at Southwestern, recalls his entire team indulging in Ed's charity. "Ed always took care of us," Johnson says. "You have to understand, it wasn't just about him giving us money. He cared about us, about our families, about how we were doing, so I don't want it to seem like he was just giving us money and that's all it was.

"But yeah, he took care of all of us. We'd have a big win and there would be something waiting for us after games, money or whatever. I've seen Ed look out for Judge. I've seen him look out for everybody, man."

CHAPTER SEVEN

The Assistant Coach

Southwestern basketball consumed my father. Starting with that 1980-81 season, he almost never missed a game. He even haunted practices with nearly the same clockwork regularity. It wasn't long before he had forged a fast friendship not only with the players, but with the coaching staff, as well.

No coach drew closer to Ed during Southwestern's heyday than Perry Watson. For most of Southwestern's decade-long dominance in the Detroit Public School League, Ed and Watson were viewed by many as inseparable. They traveled together. They took in other games together. Their families dined together. The two men talked before games and after, as much about life as about basketball. Just as he would with players, Ed often gave Watson and his wife small gifts and trinkets, bought dinners and, of course, fancy pastries.

It wasn't always that way. At first, Watson kept a close eye on Ed's interactions with his players. He learned quickly of Ed's penchant for excessive giving and immediately established himself as a moderating influence. Had he left it up to Ed, Southwestern players would've been showered with cash and Gatorade and fast food after every big win and even after a great practice. Before the 1982-83 season moved into full swing, Ed had already become a regular in post-game celebrations. He would sidle up to the game's high scorer or leading rebounder for a vigorous handshake that would leave the kid a few hundred bucks richer. Watson often had to make Ed keep his money in his pocket.

Were he a different coach from a different place and at a different time, Watson might've objected more strenuously to Ed doing even small favors for his players, let alone feeding and outright paying them after games. But Watson was a product of the same blue-collar, black-and-Latino neighborhoods in Detroit that regularly comprised Southwestern's student body. He knew that many of the boys came from some of the poorest blocks in the city. Some lived in hardscrabble neighborhoods where gangs divided between Southwestern and Western High school scrapped for turf and props. These were communities gripped by the crack cocaine epidemic of the '80s offering only dangerous ways for a kid to get a dollar or a meal. Watson knew what it took to keep a kid focused, to keep his hopes alive.

Watson saw that Ed's largesse could help stabilize and motivate players whose home lives often ranged from rocky to outright dysfunctional. Helping was one thing – exploitation was another. Watson would quickly cut Ed off if he got the sense that he was trying to take advantage of his players. On the other hand, if this guy really wanted to help these kids, then Watson wasn't going to turn him away.

From the moment Watson embraced him, Ed doted on the Southwestern players as if they were his own children. He bought coats for players like PAC 10 Hall of Famer Tarence Wheeler and future NBA standout Voshon Lenard. He purchased meals and shoes for kids like Anderson Hunt, who would later help lead University of Nevada, Las Vegas to an NCAA title. It wasn't always something big or expensive – Ed gave kids rides to and from home. After a while, his help even spread directly into some players' households, with Ed helping cover utility bills, rent and groceries. Over time, Coach Watson didn't just come to tolerate Ed's boosterism – he welcomed it, in moderation.

Ed liked the influence he wielded within the Southwestern program, and he craved a bigger role. He wanted to be more than a financial benefactor. He could have a hand in actually shaping the squad by bringing in talented players. Never one to do things in moderation, he sometimes went rogue. Case in point: Terry Mills, the can't-miss kid in Romulus.

Dad told me how he had made the first contact through Terry's father. He wanted to see if Terry might be interested in coming to Southwestern so one Sunday he drove out to Romulus to meet him, to find out if he was happy where he was. Coach Perry couldn't do that, of course, and had no idea what Ed Martin was doing.

Despite the brazen, unannounced visit, as Dad recalled to me, it was Mills' father who broached the subject. As Ed described it:

> *His father approached me. He said, 'They don't do anything for my son. They don't do anything for me. And I'd like for him to go some other place.'*
>
> *We went by the house, had a few drinks. And I told him I was going to the track at Windsor. And I said, well, 'If I win, I'll give you 10 percent of what I make.' That's what I told him. I won $2,400. I kept $2,000 myself. I gave him $400. And I think I bought a cake and some cologne. I do that a lot – the gifts.*
>
> *After I gave him the $400, he approached me again about some money. He asked me about paying rent at his house. I said, 'I'll make sure that you get $400 a month to pay your rent and something to help your house out.' I was just trying to help out Southwestern and the team. And Perry couldn't do it; you know what I mean? And I was going to.*

But when Mills' mother got wind of Ed's visit, she immediately phoned the Romulus coach, who confronted Ed about trying to lure his best player away from the program. Ed insisted that he'd only extended the conversation after Mills' father claimed he was dissatisfied. When the Romulus coach asked about Watson's role in my father's attempt, Dad assured him that the Southwestern coach didn't even know Ed had visited the home or that he had any designs whatsoever on Mills for the Prospector program.

Ed said the coach eventually wound up forgiving the transgression and later when they met face-to-face even told Ed that he envied Southwestern for having him.

> *He and I shook hands. And he told me, 'I wish I had somebody like that to help me out. Get players to do this and that.'*
>
> *I said, 'Nope. I'm just with Perry at Southwestern.'*
>
> *And we left it there.*

The incident blew over, and Watson apparently never held it against Ed. For his part, Ed just chalked it up to one in a long string of attempts he made during the '80s to help out Watson, players and their families.

"They had a great relationship, but P. Watt, he had to hold Ed back a little bit," recalled Tarence Wheeler, a former All-America guard from Southwestern who went on to star at Arizona State. "Because Eddie was a giver. And when you have 14, 15, 16-year-old young men that need so much, it is easy to get you off track in terms of your work effort, because you have been given it, you ain't earning it. Ed could afford to give it. If he wanted to, he could lace the whole team with whatever he wanted to. But with Perry, it was like, 'Let them earn it.' So I would say that Watt had to make sure that he kept it like, 'Okay, Ed, this guy is earning it.' And then he'd reward you for earning it."

Wheeler remembers vividly – and from his own personal experience – some of those moments when Watson refused to allow Ed to give anything at all to his players.

"Oh, I am positive there were times like that," Wheeler said, laughing. "I will give you an example: My senior year, man, I am top 40 or top 50 in the country. I am kind of feeling myself a little bit.

Tarence Wheeler gets his orders from Arizona State coach Bill Frieder. Frieder had gone to ASU after he was ushered out of the University of Michigan head coaching job prior to the NCAA championship run as the Wolverines went on to win the National Championship.

I came up with a little Nike All-American thing. So I got this Spanish class first hour. My tardiness wasn't really my fault, though. It was really the bus. I am on Michigan and the Boulevard. I mean I got to catch the Joy Road straight to Fort Street and then catch the Fort Street to Southwestern. Sometimes the Joy Road is full with Western kids. So I can't get on the bus. So I may be late. So the Spanish teacher, man, she waits and she only expelled me for like three tardies in September and October. Of course, she turned the paperwork in the first game of the season in December.

"Three o'clock practice we all circle up. Watt is talking about life – and I really respected these conversations because he said a lot of things that are applicable today – saying things like 'misery loves company' and 'what you do off the court controls what you do on the court.' 'Never let the little head think for the big head.' It was a lot of real-man conversations. But he also would talk about you in that situation if you screwed up.

"So, I am expelled now for three days. Perry's giving this conversation and then he goes into his stance and says, 'Damn, Wheel! Captain of the team and his ass get expelled!' He already knew why I got expelled but it was the opportunity to teach these young guys don't let this happen to you. So now, of course, after practice Ed comes about 4:30 or 5 p.m. He's ready to hook me up, too, got a little cash or whatever. But now Watt's told him what's going on. You don't get rewarded for that. And I didn't. Watt made sure of it, and Ed honored that."

There were other incidents like this that tested the limits to how far P. Watt would let Big Ed go. Their shared love of Southwestern basketball and their devotion to the players became the foundation for a close-knit friendship. Soon many nights found Watson and his wife enjoying another evening of expensive wine and a fancy meal with Ed and Hilda Martin.

The two men became so close that many people around the Southwestern community and in prep basketball circles started to believe they were related. It was an easy mistake to make, as both were wiry and light-skinned.

"At first, even I thought him and coach were related," says Flinn Hall, a former Southwestern center who now serves as principal of Romulus High School. "I thought they had to be cousins or something. But either way, Ed was family. I think that was one of the keys to the success with the Prospector family. Ed was not put out there. We didn't get into what he did, even if we knew. We were young guys. Ed was an adult. We respected what he did for us, whether it was the meals, the shoes or the money.

"For example, I will never forget the thought I had as an adult trying to explain Ed to a close friend. If one were to ask you what's

Flinn Hall called himself "an undersized center" who played for coach Perry Watson at Southwestern High School. He went on to a career in education and coaching and now serves as Principal of Romulus High School.

more important, a pair of shoes to play ball or a Big Mac? The answer is quite obvious. A pair of shoes cost $60 whereas a Big Mac cost $1. Yet when you're hungry, and I do mean really hungry, and you are not sure where your next meal is coming from, ask yourself that same question. That's Ed Martin for you – he took those very real, in-your-face pressing issues off your plate.

"Ed was one of kind. You can't do nothing but admire, respect and thank God for a man like that. Other guys tried to become a friend to the program, yet coach said no. Ed treated the All-American, the twelfth man and the water boy the same. He wasn't asking anything from us. Hell, Ed knew I wasn't going pro. I was an undersized center who just busted his butt for Perry. But he looked out for me as much as anyone.

"We didn't even need to tell each other about talking about Ed. You just knew, if you were a Southwestern guy, that Ed was family and there are things that stay between family. I say that because that is key, because that piece right there was lost later on down the road."

Hall was referring to the Michigan scandal that one day would engulf Big Ed Martin, that would literally cost my father his life. A former center for one of the only two state-championship winners that Watson ever coached, Hall considers himself the consummate

"Southwestern guy." That term was the ultimate honorific that could be applied to the long line of players – whether starters or subs – who epitomize the dynasty's trademark blend of blue-collar work ethic and deep devotion to the concept of team.

The way Flinn Hall summed it up was, "Our success was in our humbleness."

Southwestern kids battled together, protected each other. Watson taught it. They lived it. They applied it to everything concerning team, and a key ingredient in that mixture was Ed Martin's unofficial role in the program.

As a result, like many Southwestern guys who reflect on Ed's fate, Hall expresses sentiments that range from sadness to scorn. He grows melancholy when he considers what befell Ed and what he and others considered the betrayal of Ed's generosity and a betrayal of the code of respectful silence that Southwestern guys honored. When Hall and others get into how Chris Webber turned on Ed after Webber's college years, they bristle.

"Ed genuinely cared," said ex-guard Johnny Johnson. "Don't get it twisted. We weren't like those bitches who took Ed's money and then told on him. He gave us plenty, but with Ed you always knew he didn't want anything in return. He did it for everybody equally because that's how much he cared about us having what we needed. If Ed could do it for you, he did. That's how he was."

Players like Johnson and Hall say they learned about Ed's numbers hustle at some point while in high school – but neither they nor anyone else who knew ever made a big deal of it. Southwestern guys knew Ed Martin as family, and, as family, they kept whatever they knew about Ed's side hustle to themselves.

"It was just kind of like, Ed loved us and we know that," Hall said. "We loved Ed. He was family. That was it. When we were with Ed, you knew you were taken care of. You didn't have to be afraid of fighting... not just from a financial standpoint but just holistically. You knew that you were safe.

"That's what Ed meant to a lot of us – security. Not just money-wise, but in terms of helping out our families, keeping our heads up, making sure we were good all the way around. People might not understand what that means unless they've been poor or deprived like a lot of our guys were. It was important to kids like us then…"

To the players, getting to know and befriend Ed was seen as a privilege, not a relationship they were entitled to simply because they were in the program. Watson, Ed and the older players usually saw to that. Meeting Ed had become something of a rite of passage reserved only for the players whose talent and hard work had earned them spots on the varsity roster.

Anderson Hunt says he remembers seeing Ed at practices and games as early as 1982. As a pre-teen, Hunt would end classes for the day at Detroit Wilson Middle School and show up at Southwestern to marvel at Joubert and Johnson.

"The earliest I can remember seeing Uncle Ed was when I was in seventh grade," says Hunt. "My sister was in cheerleading at Southwestern, and I used to go to cheerleading practice with her. Perry kind of knew I was pretty good in basketball even back then so he let me come watch practice when I'd come up to the school. That was '82, maybe '83. I used to just watch them practice.

"I used to play baseball. I wasn't even really into basketball. I just liked watching them. They got me excited just watching. It was like, Dang man, I might have to change sports. At Southwestern on the baseball team, it was predominantly Puerto Rican and white. Basketball was all black. We might have had one Puerto Rican… Also, basketball was dominant at Southwestern. So I said man, I might as well switch up.

"So I'm there, watching practice and I see Uncle Ed for the very first time. I won't forget it: He comes walking in, with the big fur on, had these fancy-ass cowboy boots. I'm looking at him like, 'What the hell?' He was sharp, smooth. You could tell by how he carried himself he had money, but you also could tell this was a good dude, not some cat just off the street. He's giving everybody fives and everything. People are like, 'Uncle Ed, what's up?' Back then nobody knew me. I saw him that day, but I didn't get a chance to meet him."

It wasn't until years later that Hunt would finally meet the man he'd gawked at from the gym bleachers. It would have been a breach of protocol for a youngster like Hunt to have presumed to speak to Big Ed Martin. There were rules, spoken and unspoken and one of them prohibited freshmen and JV guys from presuming to approach Ed. Even when a player made it to varsity, he could not take the initiative. He must wait until Ed introduced himself, or was introduced by a coach or player, before he dared enter Ed's orbit.

Even when a relationship had been properly established, players knew better than to ask anything of Uncle Ed unless their family was really in need. Of course, Ed was so crazy about the program that it rarely took more than a few weeks of practices before he'd befriended even the newest players – and not much longer after that until he was treating them to food, pastries and the occasional hundred-dollar handshake.

"It surprised the hell out of me," said Hunt when questioned about whether he actually asked Ed for the money. "No, no, no, no. You never had to ask for nothing, unless it was an emergency. But Ed already knew. He already knew stuff was going on, even before you even told him. But nine times out of ten, you weren't asking. I don't remember asking Uncle Ed for anything. I didn't have to. He always asked, 'You need anything? You okay? Your family okay?' He was just that type of dude."

Hunt says he took his first introduction to Ed to be something of a stamp of approval. Just like getting a game jersey and a locker, meeting Uncle Ed Martin was a rite of passage, a sign that a kid had arrived as a Southwestern guy as well as a player.

"It was summer before my sophomore year," Hunt recalled. "I'd played freshman ball the year before, but had screwed up in school after the season. I'd done it on purpose because I didn't want to play baseball. Coach Watson knew it too, but I wouldn't admit it. Anyway, summer comes and he kind of forgets about the baseball thing and starts prepping me to play basketball now. I'm working out with the varsity. And that's when I finally got to meet Uncle Ed. We were in the gym, finishing practice, and he just walked over to me, shook my hand, 'What's up, young fella?' I am just looking at him like he's a star. I finally got a chance to meet The Man."

Hunt says his relationship with Ed started slowly. He'd just talk to Ed occasionally at practice. Not long afterward, Ed began to pass Hunt "pocket change." "The first time he ever gave me some money, it was $100," Hunt said. "A $100 bill."

After a few weeks, the hyper-extroverted Ed began to gravitate even more to young Hunt, a vocal and fun-loving presence himself.

"I got to playing and then got to hanging out with him, me and some of the other guys. You know, he would say, 'Man, come on over and rake my leaves.' We would rake the leaves, you know what I am saying, but the leaves would come right back down. So really that was just something for us to do. He was just looking out for me. We might all go get some lunch, play some pool. Drop us back off. We started going to the Michigan games, going out to dinner. Probably go to the bakery... the stuff was so rich. I used to tell him, 'Man, white people eat this kind of food!' Uncle Ed would be coming through with mousse, truffles, and stuff like that. I'm tellin' him, 'Man, get me a sweet potato pie!' That was Uncle Ed... first class."

Indeed, for the players who made the grade – and for the exceptional talents that Ed himself worked to draw into the Southwestern fold – the presence of Big Ed Martin gave the program something of a big-time air.

CHAPTER EIGHT

Getting into the Game

By the mid 1980s, Ed Martin was imprinting his mark on the Southwestern program. That was about the same time that NBA salaries were beginning to explode along with sneaker contracts and endorsement deals. Simultaneously, college sports was transitioning into a multi-billion-dollar, multimedia behemoth.

Cash was playing a greater role in sports than ever before, and its influence was seeping into the high school – and even youth – athletic ranks. Select Amateur Athletic Union teams already were earning reputations for doling out cash to secure the best players for summer leagues. Some college coaches, their salaries starting to swell into the millions, were desperate to justify their massive deals. They began spreading dark money around to recruits through slush funds, shadowy boosters and rogue assistants.

By the time the best players got to high school, they already knew the role that money played in amateur sports. They also knew that most under-the-table deals came with the unspoken expectation that they produce. For most of their benefactors, a player's value extended only as far as the range of his jump shot.

Antoine Joubert, who was easily the most sought-after recruit Southwestern produced during the 1980s, said he learned by his sophomore year just how high the stakes could be. "I had people coming to me all the time, trying to get me to agree to go to their school," he recalls. "I had CEOs from major corporations coming at me when I was in high school. It was crazy."

Joubert said that, after being named the nation's top player at a summer camp prior to his junior year, the pressure from recruiting offers grew even more intense. He was offered money many times to sign with one school or another. "They compete," said Joubert. "These schools all try to figure out who the best players are and they go after them. They do it now, and they were doing it back when I played."

Southwestern was one of the first high schools in the country to land an endorsement deal. At away games as well as home contests, Joubert and his teammates became known for their electrifying entrances onto the court. They had one routine that found them jogging out in their flashy Nike sweats and then stripping down to reveal sparkling new uniforms. The Prospectors sported white jerseys with blue-and-gold trim at home and deep blue with gold trim on the road. Even before their games tipped off, they looked every bit the fearsome, superior basketball machine.

In the midst of all this, Ed gave something of a soul to the quasi-professionalization of Southwestern's program.

Nobody would dare say that Southwestern wouldn't have won without Ed. The coaching genius of Perry Watson is far too obvious for anyone to go that far. Over the 11-season span from 1980-91, Watson led a program that hadn't tasted playoff success since the 1970s to nine championships in the hyper-competitive Detroit Public School League. His Prospector teams also made nine appearances in the Class A state finals championship game, winning twice.

During that time, Watson amassed an overall record of 266-22, one of the most phenomenal runs of any high-school coach ever. His teams never lost more than four games in any one season. That includes three seasons in which they saw only one loss. With his 1989-90 team, Watson posted an undefeated season. That squad featured three future NBA players in Jalen Rose, Voshon Lenard and Howard Eisley. It is widely considered to be one of the greatest high-school teams in history. To this day, some prep-hoops fanatics still contend that Watson's 1990 state champs might've been deep enough to earn an NCAA Sweet 16 berth. Other basketball powers across the country have ruled their city leagues, but very few can claim an entire decade of dominance.

It is fair, however, to say that my father added a dimension to the program that helped make Watson's demanding coaching style more palatable for the players. Watson may have held the players together on the court, but Ed was often the duct tape that helped hold together more than a few of their unstable home lives.

The two men made a dynamic duo. Ed gave where Watson would withhold. Where Ed coasted, Watson drove hard. One was relentless, the other easygoing. The blend proved instrumental in the lives of the young players.

Although Ed was never an official member of the Southwestern coaching staff, many former players credit him with being a key to their success and in helping keep their lives intact. Were it not for him, some of the athletes who would lead Southwestern during its glory years may have never even have made it onto the school's campus.

The more entrenched Ed became in the Prospectors' program, the more he did for players and their families. Beyond all the non-monetary favors and kindnesses, Ed Martin supported the program with hundreds of thousands of dollars over the eleven years he spent backing the Southwestern squads.

There are common elements along the road from a junior high wannabe to high school star to collegiate standout and ultimately to a spot in the NBA. But in other ways, each route has its unique milestones. Howard Eisley, for example, took a path that presented him with somewhat more challenges than most of his contemporaries. Not only did the steady guard have to develop his skills to a superior, attention-getting level like every other potential major-college recruit, he first had to convince his mom to let him play.

Being the son of a parent who is a devout Jehovah's Witness is not ideal if balling is your calling. For religious reasons, Eisley's mother was dead set against him playing hoops. Thank Jehovah that Detroit Public School league games were played at 4:30 p.m., directly following school. My guess is Mother Eisley was unaware Howard was playing until his senior year.

Living under the same roof with a parent and attempting to hide anything is difficult. Trying to hide from your mom the fact that you are one of the best players on the best team in the country – think *Mission: Impossible.*

Many Tuesdays, Thursdays and Saturdays, there was only one way Howard could get from practice or a game directly to Kingdom Hall, the Jehovah's Witness house of worship – that was to be chauffeured by Ed Martin. This allowed the youngster to honor his mother's requirement that he attend services while also maintaining his commitment to the team. However, during Eisley's senior year the PSL Championship Game was on Tuesday evening at the University of Detroit Mercy, located on the far Northwest side and a long way from the possibility that his mother would give him a night off from praying for playing.

That night, Eisley was locked away in his room, more brokenhearted than a teenager stood up for the prom. The game was practically minutes from tipoff and he knew there was no way his mom would let him go out and forsake his religious commitment.

That is, until the doorbell rang.

"Hello, Ms. Eisley, I'm not sure if you remember me. My name is Ed Martin."

This was not their first meeting; she knew he was associated with Southwestern's basketball program. To this day, Howard can't imagine what Dad could have said to her to change her mind. All he knows is that five minutes later, he heard Uncle Ed yell upstairs, "Howard, get your stuff! C'mon, let's go!"

Ed Martin had gotten a job done that no one else would have attempted. Eisley arrived minutes before the game began, played well, and of course, the Prospectors won.

"I respect what both those men, Perry and Ed, did at that particular time," said Tarence Wheeler, who went on to run mentorship and outreach programs in Detroit. "More than with anybody except my grandmother – who was Big Mama to the whole neighborhood – it starts with them. These two men came into my life at a critical point.

"Look, between 14 and 17 you can go either way. We had guys selling weed in school. We had guys banging. You see your situation, and my situation in particular, which was the same as a lot of guys at Southwestern. Probably Bill Jones, Voshon Lenard and Antoine Joubert were the only guys who had a father in their life, out of all those players that Perry coached. You got brothers like Jalen Rose, who ain't never met his daddy. Out of the hundreds of players that came through Southwestern, a handful had their fathers actively in their life. So as a grown man now, you really respect what those men were doing, including giving up their summers.

"I remember meeting Ed as a freshman, because I was getting noticed even then. Ed comes into the school. Antoine is getting recruited by Michigan or whatever. So we sit down and have a conversation about grades, about how important it is to stay focused on your grades. It was nothing initially about basketball. Ed never once said, 'Go to the NBA.' I never had that conversation with him. I never even heard him talk to anybody about going to the NBA. It was always, 'How you doing in school?' Then Coach would validate that so-and-so was doing good.

"We were handed a progress report every Monday morning when we entered Southwestern. Coach would be standing at the door. Every player got one, and if you didn't turn it in by Friday you weren't playing. I don't care who you were. You got your classes on there, and you had to have all your teachers sign off on what your current grade was. If they didn't sign off, you ain't playing, man."

Wheeler expressed a point heard often from former Prospector players. They were threatened with a whack from the proverbial stick from their coach P. Watt at one moment and then minutes later get a dose of empathy and some sweet carrots from Uncle Ed Martin.

"I am telling you," Wheeler went on, "from my freshman year to my senior year, there wasn't a time my quarterly report card came and if my grades were right, Ed would have $100 or $200 for me. It was just 'Hey, good job,' a motivating factor.

"Then you go on to sickness, or when you are down or when lights were getting cut off. You heard about people about to get evicted. Ed was always there for guys. Man, I could tell you a hundred stories about what this man did. Times I needed Robitussin or lunchmeat or orange juice, and Ed was knocking on the door at midnight.

"I remember we were about to play Northern (Detroit Northern High School) for the PSL championship at Cobo Hall. We were off that week of school, and I am sick as a dog. Ed came to my house three times that week with medicine, orange juice, and food. Not just for me. He gave my grandmother bags of groceries, too. He didn't have to do that, man. This is something that he just did. We didn't call Ed. He must have talked to Coach and Coach was like, 'Wheel is sick.' He did for me, he did for everybody."

When former players would reflect on the influence my father had on their life, they spoke less about his help with money and gifts than about incidents that might seem small to other people but that made an indelible impression on them. Time and again they would bring up how Ed Martin had taken charge when there was no one else around to step forth to make something happen.

"The most amazing thing that I had seen Eddie do," Wheeler

said, "was just on an aha! moment for me. We were coming home from a state tournament game in a little town named Charlotte, Michigan. The game was over late. The restaurant was closed. The guy was sweeping the floor, man. Eddie knocked, talked to the guy. He was like, 'Open this damn restaurant.' The next thing, the lights are coming on, burgers were cooking and we were eating. I had never seen a black man do that before. You know what I mean? Never ever.

"And then there's the story of Doyle Callahan, who wasn't even a Southwestern guy. You want to know about Ed Martin? Think about the story of Doyle Callahan."

Indeed, while the tales of Ed's devotion to Southwestern kids abound, his charity to Doyle Callahan illustrates how long a reach there was to my father's generosity. Callahan was a prep player in the mid-'80s who blossomed into a freshman sensation some 54 miles northeast of Detroit, in the historic, mid-sized city of Port Huron.

After leading Port Huron High in his freshman year, Callahan was being hailed as one of the state's best upcoming talents. He had led the Big Reds to the team's best record in 34 seasons, 15-7. Port Huron planned on riding him to postseason success for the next three years. But Dad and the guys at Southwestern had other intentions.

And after a while, so did Doyle Callahan.

Not long after his freshman season ended, Callahan accompanied one of his coaches to a state playoff game at the old Jenison Field House in East Lansing, where Earvin "Magic" Johnson used to dazzle the nation for the Michigan State Spartans. The Prospectors were among teams battling in that tournament featuring yet another stellar lineup that included a young Anderson Hunt.

Callahan, who knew some of the Southwestern players from tournaments, camps and offseason pickup games, watched with amazement as the Prospectors tore through that night's opponent.

As he sat in the stands marveling at Southwestern's suffocating defense and punishing offensive style, he began to realize just how badly he wanted to be a part of something like that.

Sure, Callahan had been The Man from the moment he stepped on the Port Huron High campus, but he also was the youngest of his team's pillars. His friends and best teammates all were graduating. Plus, life wasn't easy at home. His mom was a double amputee. Money was tight. Callahan wanted at least a chance at something better, and for him Southwestern represented his best path to that opportunity.

"It was just amazing to watch Southwestern," Doyle Callahan recalled. "There were so many of the guys that I knew and who I wanted to play with. I had to at least talk to them.

"So, after the game, I told my coach that I was going to the bathroom. But really, I snuck into the Southwestern locker room. That's where I saw Anderson Hunt, who I knew. Me and Hunt were just standing around talking. I'm telling him how excited I was to watch them play; he's telling me how he hadn't played in the game that night because the team forgot his game shorts. And then we start talking about how cool it would be if I could play with them.

"I'm not thinking it could happen. I live in Port Huron, right? But I did think it was a cool idea. Me, as part of that team. Wow! So then Hunt walks me over to meet his coach. Perry already knew who I was, so all he said was hello and told me to give Anderson my number.

"Then all of a sudden, this older guy walks in. He's wearing this nice sweat suit and an even nicer watch. He looked like money to me. He introduced himself as Ed Martin."

Before Callahan could introduce himself, Dad cut him off. "He's smiling from ear to ear as he's shaking my hand, and he tells me, 'Oh, I know who you are. It's a real pleasure to meet you,'" Doyle remembered. "And the way he said it, you knew he meant it.

It was a nice feeling."

Doyle Callahan says that, unlike Watson, Ed made no secret of the team's desire to import him from Port Huron. Stocky, tough, and possessed of a sniper's eye with his jumper, the 6-foot-4 guard would be an ideal cog in the prep machine Watson had been assembling. However, Watson wasn't the sort of coach who obsessed over players not already in his program. If he could land you, great; if not, the Prospectors would roll on.

"Watson really didn't have much to say to me at all," Callahan said. "I knew he would welcome me if I came, but he wasn't going to go out of his way to get me to come. That's not the kind of coach he was. He didn't chase players, and he didn't kiss your ass. He was real calm about everything. I don't think I talked to him again after we talked at the game. Even if he wanted you to play for him, he wasn't going to act all crazy about it."

Ed, on the other hand, never had been one to hide his enthusiasm for sports talent. After years in the stands and on the sidelines at practices, Ed had evolved into more than just a loquacious booster who threw cash around to celebrate wins and aid young men and their families. Along the way, he had become an unofficial recruiter for the Prospectors, using his charm and flash to further underscore the cachet Watson had built with win after win. No surprise then, that even as the young sharpshooter Doyle Callahan filed out of Jenison that night, he was making plans to lure him to Detroit.

After meeting Ed that night, Callahan said, he spoke to him often during the ensuing summer. My father called him weekly to check up on his conditioning, his diet, his home life. It didn't take long before Dad's constant encouragement helped Callahan solidify his dreams of playing alongside his friends at Southwestern into a reality.

Once he had made up his mind to bolt to Southwestern, Callahan said, he didn't tell anyone at Port Huron about his decision.

Only Ed and a precious few of his future Southwestern teammates knew of his intentions. He knew that his coach, Ed Peltz, wouldn't be pleased. But he also knew moving to Detroit would be the best thing for his game – and his grades.

"I really wanted to go to college, man," he explained. "And I knew that I had a much better chance of doing that if I played for Perry and Southwestern than playing up in Port Huron." So, rather than announce his choice to what would be a devastated Port Huron team, Callahan quietly plotted with Ed to engineer his escape.

Here was Dad's plan: Before the start of classes in the fall he would drive to Port Huron, pick up Callahan and take him to live at Callahan's grandfather's house on Detroit's west side. Ed promised that he would move Callahan's family not long after. Doyle could hardly believe his ears when Ed first floated the idea, but he heard from other players that he should never doubt Ed's commitment to the team. If Uncle Ed said he'd do something, Doyle Callahan could take it to the bank.

Callahan said he tried to keep his transfer to Southwestern a secret, but Peltz heard about his intentions. He did not take the news well.

"I have talked to Doyle briefly and he said he wasn't happy playing in Port Huron," Peltz told the *Times Herald*, the city's daily newspaper. "I really don't know the reason he left... I really think Doyle could have made a name for himself in Port Huron. He would have been a player the young black kids could look to."

According to Callahan, his split with Peltz and the Big Reds was far less civil. In fact, it was almost hostile.

"In Port Huron, the school year started before it did in Detroit, so while my friends are all showing up for school, I'm nowhere around," he recalled. "I'm still at home in the projects. But the rumors are flying.

"The coach is hearing that I'm out. So he calls the house: 'Let me speak to your mom.' My mom gets on the phone and I hear her like, 'What? I owe you what?'"

Callahan said Coach Peltz showed up at his house minutes later, threatening to take his family to court.

"He was pissed," Callahan said. "He's like, 'Doyle owes me money, shoes... this isn't the last time you'll be hearing from me!'

"I had been smart enough to recruit some other guys over the summer, some really good guys, and I was hoping that having them would smooth things over for my Port Huron coach. But it didn't. He wanted me."

It didn't matter. Callahan was firm on his decision to leave. He said Peltz hadn't sent any players to major colleges in the years before Doyle arrived, and he didn't want to squander four years with no chance of playing at the next level.

Any sympathy Doyle Callahan may have felt for his Port Huron team evaporated as soon as Peltz began demanding money and threatening to take his family to court. Until that incident, Doyle had always believed that his coach had only his best interest as a student-athlete at heart. "I told him straight up, 'I'm gone, man,'" Callahan said.

A few days before classes were to begin in Detroit Public Schools, Callahan found himself standing with his family in front of his house in the projects of Port Huron. It was the day he was scheduled to leave for his grandfather's house. Family, friends, even distant acquaintances had shown up to see whether this big-talking recruiter from Detroit actually would make good on his word.

"I remember it so well," said Callahan. "It was like the *Chariots of Fire* movie. Everybody in the neighborhood is at my house, all my boys. We're standing around talking when all of sudden that big green Benz pulls up. It was amazing! Here I was in high school, about to roll off to Detroit like I was some big-time NBA guy or whatever. Ed didn't just show up like he said he would. He showed up in style! Everybody was pumped. My boys were jumping up and down like, 'We can't believe this!'"

Callahan remembers how Ed was grinning, shaking hands all around, reveling in the moment just like everyone else. He chatted up Callahan's mother for several minutes, then cracked a few jokes with the neighborhood guys, whose numbers seemed to suddenly triple the instant Ed's Mercedes rolled up.

"His charisma was unlike anyone else's," Callahan said. "He was just a beautiful, genuine person. I mean, I haven't met another man like that in my life. I just haven't. People were crying. I mean, it was really special."

And with that, Callahan was gone.

That's how it went if you were a Prospector ballplayer in the 1980s and early '90s. As long as Big Ed Martin was around, you didn't want for anything, unless Coach Watson said otherwise.

Months after moving Callahan to Detroit, Ed went back to Port Huron and moved Callahan's mother and other relatives to Detroit to be with him. For the next three years, Ed doted on the Callahan family as if they were his own, making sure that his mother and siblings wanted for nothing.

After Callahan's Southwestern career ended, Ed moved Callahan's family right back to Port Huron, just as he had promised. Ironically, Doyle rejected offers from major universities and chose to play at tiny Washburn University in Topeka, Kansas, where he graduated with a degree in communications.

Looking back, Callahan says, "Never once did Ed Martin ask for anything in return."

CHAPTER NINE

Give and Go

It was one single phone call, just one of many. But it changed everything.

Before that fateful phone call from Chris Webber in the spring of 1989, Ed Martin expected nothing from the once-in-a-generation superstar. As Big Ed had done for so many kids, he simply gave without expectations. He did that because he could. Also, perhaps at some deep emotional level, it helped him to heal his own childhood wounds. And yes, he opened his wallet in part because he was driven by his own personal desire to gain entre into exclusive groups that otherwise had been closed to him for most of his adult life.

After that phone call from Chris Webber, things would never be the same again.

In the era before Michael Jordan hit the NBA, the league's highest-paid player was making $1 million a year. Many longtime basketball fans remember Earvin "Magic" Johnson signing a 25-year, $25 million contract with the Los Angeles Lakers. Add in the shoe contract with Converse for $200,000 – chump change by later standards – and that was as good as it gets.

Lofty numbers indeed. But very few ballplayers were making

more money than Ed Martin before he and Chris Webber crossed paths. Earning a legal $1.2 million a year before taxes was in the same ballpark as what Ed brought in through his multiple revenue streams. Dad had been in the numbers game more than twenty years. Combine his on-the-books salary with his off-the-books hustle and his total income rivaled the highest-paid NBA player in 1984.

However, everything soon changed after Michael "Air" Jordan was drafted third overall by the Chicago Bulls in 1984 and visionary Nike pioneered the coming dominance of the mega-endorsers.

Nike might have had a name people were unsure how to pronounce but they certainly had a game plan. It didn't take long before it was a whole new ball game and a highly lucrative one for players fortunate enough to be just coming onto the scene. From 1984 to 1987, aided by a major assist from Nike, earning potential for a college star entering the NBA expanded exponentially.

Ed Martin, a savant with figures and finance, took notice. So, in the spring of 1989 when he got the call from Webber, he was immediately interested.

Dad probably was more accustomed to taking the random or unexpected phone call than most people. Decades of operating in the shadows prepared him well. Still, I never will forget the afternoon Dad called me to break down the odd, yet not really surprising, conversation he'd just had with Webber.

"Son, I just got a call from Chris asking if he could come over and talk," Ed told me. "Whatever it is, he didn't want to have the conversation on the phone. His voice was slightly nervous and I could tell he had something to ask. You know, like something he needs to get off his chest."

Dad made sure I was available to sit in. He knew that when a potential business matter was to be discussed and can't be written down, it's a good idea to have another set of ears in the room.

In contrast to what sportswriter Mitch Albom has written or

said many times, there indeed was another person in that meeting between my father and Webber—and I was that person. Albom has consistently written that we can never know what exactly happened between the two because Ed is no longer with us and Chris won't talk. There is some truth to that statement. I was not present for every Martin-Webber interaction, but I most definitely was at that very critical meeting because Ed Martin sensed that would be a particularly meaningful encounter.

In the mid-afternoon of an early spring day, Chris Webber came to our place on Fairway Drive. Alone. He was wearing his customary basketball-related logo-ed gear. Dad and I, as much curious as we were nervous, were waiting for him.

After greeting him, we made our way over to my father's favorite talking area, the space between the living room and the pool table, one of Dad's favorite pieces of furniture. Webber had to be at least 0-for-10 against my dad on the green felt.

Next to the pool table was an island bar. Two bar stools and matching chairs were positioned on either side of the bar. As Ed always did, he sat in one of the two chairs on the window side of the bar to have a view of the 36-hole golf course just beyond in his backyard.

Over the years, reflecting on that meeting, it always strikes me how calm the sixteen-year-old Chris Webber appeared. After some small talk, he shifted to his agenda with a statement of the obvious.

"You know, both my parents work," he said. "Yet we rarely have enough because there are five kids."

Chris stared straight into Dad's eyes. "You also know that I am going to make it."

"Yep, I do know that," my father replied.

"And when I do, you know that I am going to take care of you."

"OK. That would be great," Ed said.

"So I am hoping we can have more assistance. Because when I make it, we are going to look out for you."

Without a moment's pause, Dad agreed that, yes, he would provide additional assistance to Chris and his family.

So there it was. Out in the open. On the table. Not a shred of ambiguity.

As if to put a double stamp of confirmation on the deal that had just been struck, Chris said it again, "Thank you, man. You know I am going to look out for you,"

Dad looked at him and nodded. "I know you will," he responded.

We all stood, exchanged hugs and started toward the door as Dad and I gave each other a look. We realized how much everything had just changed. How much the stakes had been raised. For everybody.

After Chris was gone, Dad and I were silent for a time. Then he said, "Do you have any doubt he will make it to the league?"

My answer was a simple "No."

As I reflect on Ed's life and the decisions that shaped it, this brief meeting was pivotal. When you consider that Webber was the first kid he aligned himself with outside of Southwestern, as a benefactor with no controls or restrictions, Ed Martin had put himself on a fateful path.

This time there was no stern Coach Perry Watson to moderate the flow of assistance. Here was a massive sure-thing talent who had taken the initiative to ask for more. Chris Webber had come to my father boldly, shamelessly, with a straight-out request for increased financial help in exchange for a future payback. At that moment Big Ed Martin's relationship with a high school basketball player changed from being a benefactor to becoming something much less pure. The irony was inescapable. The deep-pocketed booster, Big Ed Martin, was being compromised by a supposedly innocent high school basketball player.

Not that my father hesitated even slightly to accept the Webber proposition. NBA salaries and endorsement deals had skyrocketed so dramatically that the possible future payouts for Ed Martin were beyond substantial – they were irresistible.

Ed Martin held up his end of the bargain and, as was his practice, went well beyond.

Over the next three years, there were so many incidents that illuminate how both parties performed, leaving no doubt there was no ambiguity in the relationship. It soon became clear that Chris's father, Deacon Mayce Webber, fully understood the commitments on both sides of the pact that Chris had proposed and my father had accepted. I didn't have to take that on faith from a second-hand account from my father because I was on the scene time and again to hear for myself.

Cases in point: The Fab Five's back-to-back Final Four appearances.

In 1992, to accommodate attendance by all the Webbers at U-M's much-anticipated appearance in the Twin Cities, we borrowed a fully loaded cargo van from my mother-in-law, Virginia Grier. I drove Chris's immediate family in that van, while my father drove Deacon Webber. Of course there were all the expected expenses, and many more besides, while only the deep pockets of Big Ed Martin were tapped.

In some ways, that first experience transporting and hosting the Webber family was a warmup act for the second Final Four, in 1993 in New Orleans. More than that, it produced an additional layer of indulgence and expense that the first Final Four did not have. Big Ed Martin bought plane tickets for the entire Webber family while I took the train. At both events, the Webbers relied on food and lodging from Ed, and game tickets as well as thousands of dollars of pocket money, all from Ed, always from Ed.

As I play back the conversations in my head, I remain genuinely impressed how prophetic – and seemingly well thought-out and calculated – the Deacon's words have proved to be over time. He was emphatic that his son was going to look out for us when he "made it":

"You are going to be surprised what Chris is going to do for you."

And so, over the next six years, Ed Martin, a man who was serious about numbers, calculated that he gave Webber, his father and his mother some $450,000.

Yes, Mayce Webber was right about one thing. When Chris Webber reneged on the deal he himself had proposed, when the entire Webber family backed away from a solemn obligation they invited and incurred, yes their benefactor Ed Martin was surprised. And disappointed. And made to feel he had been the victim of a betrayal he himself would never inflict on another person.

Many years later, there were days when Dad and I were frustrated and one of us would just blurt out, "You are going to be surprised what Chris is going to do for you." Then we would look at each other and laugh.

We would look back on incidents like the one in 1989, when Dad took Chris Webber to one of metro Detroit's fanciest restaurants. This was the summer before his junior year of high school. Dad realized Chris was a high profile, can't miss-talent at Detroit Country Day, an elite private school in the Beverly Hills suburb. Dad knew Chris would have many opportunities to dine at fine restaurants and he wanted to ensure that the young man had proper etiquette.

Of course young Chris could read a menu and place an order. But did he know which utensil to use and when, why there were so many glasses for each person, or what to do with the napkin on the charger?

One evening Ed took him to a restaurant in the Ritz-Carlton Dearborn hotel. A jacket was required for the dinner seating; Webber left home without one. Ed knew the restaurant would have jackets available, so no big deal. When he picked Webber up, he never said a word.

Nonetheless, the two enjoyed a delicious meal while Ed talked Chris through the proper use of the tableware. When the meal was finished and it was time to leave, Ed noticed that a duck entrée was one of the specials of the day. He knew that Webber's mother absolutely loved duck, so he ordered the special to go for her to enjoy at home.

Dad didn't really have to give of his own time for years, routinely two or three times a week, he delivered dinners to the entire Webber family. Instead, he could have just handed the Webbers the cash to dine at The Van Dyke Place or wherever they liked. Instead of personally buying and delivering groceries, it would have been much easier and less draining on him to simply give them even more money.

Just as he could have strolled out of the Ritz Carlton dining room rather than wait for a special duck dinner to be prepared so he could personally deliver it to Mrs. Webber.

For Ed Martin, whenever he had the choice, it was more meaningful for him to be thoughtful, to give of his time rather than of his money. I believe my father invested so much time and money with the Webbers over six years because that expressed how important they were to him.

My father might have thought of himself as an independent operator, but he would never have been able to accomplish the good things he did if he had not been married to a woman who was wise and intuitive in her own right – not to mention forgiving and long-suffering. Patient as she was, Hilda Martin was neither naive nor oblivious. She often let my father know he was providing too much too soon for these young men. Any kid who has everything handed to him will never appreciate all that is given, she insisted. How prophetic that turned out to be, especially in the case of Chris Webber.

When your life partner and most trusted confidant emphatically spells out the correct approach for you to take, why do you not listen? "Why do you have to do so much?" she would ask. Mom wasn't saying don't do anything. She wasn't even saying do no more. She was just advising Ed to close down the valve a little.

There were questions for which she never got a satisfying answer.

Did we have to let Webber drive our car to his prom? Did Ed have to throw the graduation party for Chris at one of Detroit's fanciest hotels in one of their nicest rooms, or pick up the heavy tab at a five-star restaurant for his college announcement part? Did Martin money have to subsidize his off-campus apartment in his sophomore year at U-M? Did Chris Webber need not one but two accounts so he could shop for sports and dress apparel and just sign for it? And did he really need that lavish cash handshake every week?

There are things in life that can't be measured by a string of numbers after a dollar sign. Some people feel that those non-monetary things are all that truly matter in life. Despite all that my father did both *for* money and *with* money, he was such a person.

Because of the nature of my father's dealings, both above board and below, there is much in this book about business, about his affinity for numbers, about cash coming in and flowing out. To my father, cash was important only in that it was a means to an end. For a man who was so sophisticated in wheeling and dealing with large amounts of cash, he was extraordinarily naive about how money was viewed by others. To many, money was apparently an end in itself.

Ed Martin had seen thousands of basketball games and countless horse races. He knew that the numbers on the gym scoreboard or track tote board instantly separated the winners from the losers. But somehow he believed that a person should never extend that easy calculation into personal relationships. A man just doesn't lord it over others simply because he had a bigger bank account. And Ed Martin certainly never would have sullied his own reputation or lost respect for himself by reneging on his word. Never would he have walked away from any kind of debt and most certainly not from a debt of honor.

This is why it damaged him in so many ways when Chris Webber betrayed his trust.

Webber hit the pros in 1993. That year he got a bonus of $12 million, just to sign the contract. That was on top of his salary and his shoe contract. With just a sliver of his bonus, Chris could have reimbursed Dad for all the assistance he received. If that had happened, end of story. Perhaps that is precisely what the young Chris Webber who asked for more of my father's help would have done.

But there are forks in the road of life and you can seldom tell if you've taken the right path until you are already too far along. For six years, the Martins travelled with Chris Webber on his path from high school and two years of college to the brink of a lucrative NBA career.

Supplying cash and gifts wasn't the only purpose Ed served for Webber. On occasion, Big Ed also provided other favors and services for Webber – some noble, others downright unsavory.

Dad's loyalty to Webber never was more apparent than after the Wolverines lost the 1992-93 NCAA title game to the University of North Carolina Tar Heels following Webber's infamous timeout gaffe. The mistake itself is one of the most fabled and embarrassing moments in college basketball history.

On April 5, 1993, playing in their second straight NCAA championship game, the Wolverines were down 73-71 with 11 seconds left. Webber brought the ball up the court but was met by a smothering half-court trap. With the Heels pawing at the ball, a desperate Webber attempted to call a timeout. He had forgotten that coach Steve Fisher had told the team during their previous timeout that they had none left. The blunder led to a technical foul that essentially ended the game in a North Carolina victory.

After the loss, Webber was despondent. He already had disclosed to Ed the likelihood that he was going pro after that season, so he was particularly determined to bring a title back to Ann Arbor. That his team had lost stung deeply enough; that he had committed such a glaring error down the stretch devastated the emotionally fragile man-child.

Webber went out on the town later that night and got severely drunk in an effort to numb the pain of the loss. Knowing his delicate state of mind, Ed suggested that my friends and I keep an especially close eye on him.

As he was leaving a club, an inebriated and melancholy Webber stopped and slumped to the ground. Sprawled out there, he began to sob.

Onlookers gathered around. One guy was carrying a large professional-looking camera. When we saw the camera aimed at Chris, we instinctively positioned ourselves in front of the lens. While I blocked the camera's view, Geoffrey Craig, a friend who had followed me out of the club, snatched the paparazzo's camera. The rest of us rushed to Chris, lifted that big body up and carried him to a car. Given the circumstances of the loss, a photo of a drunken Chris blubbering on the sidewalk would have spread far and wide the next day.

While Webber was at Michigan, Ed took his philanthropy toward him to ever-higher levels. Although Webber technically was required to live in the dorms during his freshman year, Ed rented him a spacious apartment in Ann Arbor. He bought him clothes, groceries, furniture and jewelry. Whatever Webber wanted during his time at U-M, Ed made sure he had it.

He always let Webber's parents, Doris and Mayce, know when he did something for their son. He didn't ask their permission, per se. Ed was far too impulsive and compliant to Chris' wishes to do that. But if Chris wanted my father to buy him clothes, or a necklace, or even food, Ed usually made sure his parents approved—even if they had been made aware after the fact. If Dad wanted to take Webber to a restaurant, or rent a hotel room for him and his friends, Mayce or Doris would get a call letting them know Ed's "godson" was all right.

Ed could recall only one instance when he wanted to do something for Webber and didn't notify his mother and father.

That was when he bought him his first nice set of wheels.

Back in high school, Webber was given a 1980s Chevrolet Corsica as a sixteenth birthday gift. For a lot of high school kids, especially the children of working-class black parents in Detroit, any car would have viewed as a blessing. But for Webber, the Corsica was far too small. A full 6-foot-9 after graduating from high school, Webber had to contort himself just to get in and out of the vehicle. Just to get in, he needed to fold his knees nearly up to his chin and his oversized hands struggled with the controls. Just as bad, the car was aged and ugly. Webber desperately wanted to upgrade.

And all it took was a passing mention, as my father recalled years later:

> *Chris wanted a car real bad. One day I asked him, 'Chris, your parents—will they let you have a car?' He said, 'Yes, they'll let me have it.' So I didn't go to them and ask them.*
>
> *Anyway, I drove up and down Woodward Avenue, and up and down Telegraph Road, looking at all the dealerships, trying to find a cheap car for him to drive. Then one day I was leaving Ford out on Rotunda Drive, and I saw this car. It just had to be a good car. It was beautiful! A Ford Bronco II, tricked out, visor, nice wheels. I saw it and said, 'Boy, that might be just the car I want!'*
>
> *So I stopped and talked to the guy on the lot, and he told me it'd be $16,500 or something like that. 'I have to*

sell it,' he kept saying. 'These used cars have got to move. I need to get rid of it.'

I told him, 'Well, my godson is Chris Webber' – I was hoping he liked sports – 'and I'm looking for a car for him. Maybe I'll check and see if he's interested in it.'

Soon as I said it, the guy's face lit up and his voice got real excited. 'Chris Webber?' Yeah, I'd love to meet him! Why don't you bring him by?'

So I went and got Chris. I told him I saw the car we've been looking for and I wanted to take him by and let him look at it. I told him that people at the lot – it was a guy named Beauchamp and his wife – wanted to meet him, and he said, 'Great.' We went by there because he wanted to. I wasn't twisting his arm or manipulating the kid. He was a good young man. He was working hard, had done well, and I was trying to give him what he wanted.

I took him inside and introduced him to them. They really seemed to enjoy getting a chance to meet him. Chris seemed OK with it, too. And the truck? He loved the truck.

So while we're there, I pulled him aside and made a plan. 'I got $5,000 on me. I will give you $5,000 now on this. I'll get the rest and pay off what you owe on it.'

I told Chris I'd borrow the rest of it from my brother, but really I went to the bank and got a loan for $12,000. After that, I went back and paid off the thing after a year.

That day, I gave the man the money I had, we picked up the truck, then brought it back home. When we got back, I said, 'I'm going to put it in your name.'

But suddenly, Chris said, 'Wait 'til tomorrow,' or something like that. So I'm thinking Chris might not have told his parents we were getting this. I don't know for sure, 'cause he told me that he had talked to them and it was OK. Now, he's coming back and saying, 'Don't put it *in my name… I have to leave it over at your house. And I'll just drive it for a while but I'll get it straightened out.'*

He never got it straightened out.

I think his parents wouldn't let him take it. So we left it out front at my house. And he would come over to the house, leave the Corsica, then get the truck whenever he wanted to go out. He'd drive it, come back, leave the truck at my house, get into his Corsica and go home. I guess his parents didn't know it. That lasted about a month. I ended up keeping the truck. But I bought it for Chris.

I didn't get into it with his parents about it, but that was pretty dumb to me. I really thought they were going let Chris have the truck. It didn't dawn on me until afterwards. I think they were afraid somebody would see him riding, see that I brought him this truck, and think he was getting this from me. I don't think it was planned this way, but maybe it was. Maybe Chris was trying to get over on me. I don't know.

Ed's relationship with Webber continued this way throughout his time at Michigan. If he wanted or needed a favor, he always called Ed. After games, Ed would usually meet Webber in the locker room, back on campus or at the apartment Ed rented for him, where he would hand him a few hundred dollars or more in "pocket change." Webber wasn't flashy, at least not on campus, so he and Ed usually were able to fly under the radar when it came to cash and other gifts.

They both were well aware of the consequences if they ever were discovered. Webber would lose his eligibility instantly. And Ed could be brought up on criminal charges.

Even so, Ed insisted that those closest to Webber knew full well what Ed was doing for the superstar player. And back then, when money was flying and Ed was footing every tab that came their way, nobody seemed to mind.

I would tell Deacon Webber, 'I gave Chris this... I gave him that.' They knew everything: the clothes, the parties, the money. They let me do everything... as long as it didn't show up.

There were no objections. When I bought the clothes, they were there. They knew I bought his class ring. Somebody had to buy it! They knew what was going on. Deacon Webber did. I didn't discuss every little thing with Sister Webber, I really didn't. But the father, he knew everything that was going on.

And I never asked for anything in return. Deacon Webber borrowed $400 or $500 dollars from me once when they did some work to their house, and he paid me that back. That's the only thing he ever paid me back.

I gave thousands of dollars to Chris' parents. Not Chris. His parents! Deacon never straight up asked me for money, though. No, he would always say it like this: 'I ain't got no money, but we need this. We need food. We need a ham for this trip. We need tickets for this.'

And I'd just go and get it.

If he went with me to the racetrack and I won, I'd give him some money. I'd pay for everything when we went out. I took them to some of the best restaurants. I always made sure they had a good time. I loved Chris, and I figured these people were like my family, too.

When Michigan played Ohio State during Chris' freshman year, his daddy didn't have any money so I gave him like three hundred dollars there. When the Fab Five went to New Orleans and Minnesota during their back-to-back championship appearances, Deacon Webber didn't have any money. I gave him a thousand when they went to New Orleans. When they drove to Minnesota, I gave him another thousand, when he had no car. I gave this to Dea-

con, not to Chris.

That's what I mean. If Deacon Webber needed anything, I got it for him. We took several road trips to Chris' collegiate games, and at those times I didn't have to give him money, 'cause I'd just spend it. Like when we went to Purdue, whatever we'd get, I paid for it. I bought whatever he ate. When we went to the pizza place, I bought seven pizzas so everybody would have enough. I bought him beer and stuff. Whatever we did, Deacon Webber got.

But he never did ask. He didn't have to ask for a loan. He'd say he didn't have nothing, and I'd give it to him. That way he didn't have to pay it back. He was slick.

But for all the impropriety in Ed's relationship with the Webbers, few of Ed's favors raised eyebrows about possible violations of NCAA regulations. While much of what Ed did on Webber's behalf might be viewed as innocuous, there was at least one time when Dad's devotion took a much darker turn.

One day in 1993, during Webber's sophomore year, Ed's phone rang. Webber was on the other end, but Ed could barely make out anything he was saying. From the tone of his voice it was obvious there was a problem.

"What's the matter, Chris?" Ed asked, more than once.

Finally Chris calmed down enough to be coherent.

"My girl is pregnant," Webber said. "She's talking like she's going to have the baby, but I don't want any kids. I don't know what to do."

Ed listened for a few more minutes, then broke in.

"Don't worry about it," he told Chris. "I'll take care of it." With that, he hung up the phone.

The next day, Ed called a couple tough guys he knew from the streets. Few modern-day numbers men are themselves gangsters, or need to be. But one can't be in that business without knowing people from all walks of life. My father was no exception. He had friends he could call upon if and when situations got too rough for him alone.

Now he was calling in these brothers on his godson's behalf.

Several days later, after my dad had furnished the address, two bruisers drove up to the apartment where Webber's girlfriend lived. Given the time of day, she most likely was in class. They walked into the building and quickly identified her apartment unit.

Standing outside her door, the thugs wedged the open end of a balloon underneath her door. Inside the balloon was more than a quart of gasoline. One of them then stomped on it, sending the gas spraying inside the apartment. Then they shoved a note under the door.

"Next time," it read, "we will light it."

Not long after, Webber called my father and told him his girlfriend had gotten an abortion. He thanked Ed profusely.

Now, let me state for the record: that was seriously wrong. There is no way anyone should treat any person that way. Orchestrating that reprehensible incident with Chris' girlfriend was indefensible. And a chilling example of how far Uncle Ed Martin would go to protect his "godson" Chris Webber.

In all of Ed's many dealings with hundreds of players, terrorizing Webber's girlfriend into getting an abortion easily rates as the lowest my father ever stooped for anyone, as far as I am aware. I deplore what my father did and it hurts me to recount it. But it was an important event in my father's life and in my promise to my mother that I would tell the whole Ed Martin story it had to be included, even though, mercifully, she never knew about it.

In 1993 and 1994, there were several major milestones in the professional basketball career of Chris Webber and in my father's relationship with him. Choices that Webber made on those two occasions became millstones that hung around my father's neck until the day he died.

I remember the exact moment when Chris Webber first communicated unmistakably that he had no intention of living up to the very commitment he himself had asked for years earlier. It was a summer day in 1993 after Webber was drafted by the NBA's Orlando Magic, the first sophomore to be a No. 1 draft pick since Magic Johnson. Webber was instantly traded to the Golden State Warriors to begin a 15-year career in which he would make over

Despite the bitter irony of the words on the poster behind them, Chris Webber and Ed Martin shared many good times, many smiles

$200 million in salaries, endorsements and other compensation.

He pulled up to Dad's house in a car with three of his friends. His boys stayed in the vehicle while he walked into a house he had visited many times. He was carrying an old bank bag. He set the bag down on the table. He obviously was going to stay only long enough to exchange a few pleasantries. As quickly as he had come, he was gone.

I looked at the bag, not knowing that in a few years I would see that bag again.

We opened the bag immediately and counted the money. Unbelievable. So we counted the cash again. And then twice more. Each time we got the same result—$38,200. Why such an odd amount? A few months later, I learned that Webber actually got $40,000 from the bank, but gave his three running buddies $600 each before he got out of the car. Perhaps doling out that $1,800 shouldn't be surprising, not if you've convinced yourself that you didn't owe Uncle Ed Martin money after all. That easily justifies taking money earmarked for your long-time benefactor and handing it off to someone else.

An old bank bag containing less than a tenth of Webber's obligation left no doubt that the moment Chris got his NBA signing bonus and his Nike contract, he no longer felt beholden to his debts to the Martins.

Why it happened will forever be a perplexing mystery to my family. Webber had asked, the Martins had provided. He promised, we believed. We honored our part of the deal, and then some. From the moment that Webber came to us and asked us to elevate our support to him and his family, every single time he called over those six years we answered.

We never pressured Webber to take care of us (as he and his father had often and clearly committed to) as soon as he hit the league because at that time Dad's pockets were still full.

After that remarkable visit, over the next several months we reached out to him many times. He never answered our calls.

Then, early in 1994, during Webber's NBA rookie season with the Golden State Warriors, Mom and Dad finally managed to schedule a trip to visit him in California. After coordinating the dates with Chris, they flew to the West Coast to enjoy a mini-vacation and celebrate his success. To them, this was a joyous occasion, an opportunity to share quality time with a young man they saw grow and develop over the last six years. I am sure they had a huge sense of pride, and deservedly so, as contributors to his life's journey. Not many people can say they made such an indelible impact at a crucial stage in the life of pro basketball's No. 1 overall pick.

After their four-hour flight from Detroit, Mom and Dad rented a car and drove another hour or so to Webber's home in the mountains. When they got there, they were surprised to discover you could not drive directly onto his property: there was a huge gate that had to be opened before one could enter. Webber hadn't mentioned this to them.

They spoke with the gentleman who operated the gate. "We're Ed and Hilda Martin from Detroit," Dad announced. "We're in town to visit our godson for a few days."

The guard explained that Webber was not home, nor was the guard aware they were coming. But that's no problem, he quickly added: give him a minute and he would put a call in to Chris.

Fifteen minutes later, the gatekeeper returned to their car, leaned in and informed them that he had spoken to Webber. "He asked if you could maybe go shopping or grab a bite to eat, and he will be home in a few hours," the guard said. He added that Chris did not give his approval for them to enter the estate and wait for him. They really had no option but to entertain themselves for a few hours and return.

Food fancier that he was, Ed already had researched area restaurants he wanted to try. He also had identified shopping prospects for Hilda. Although they were stunned and dejected by Webber's behavior, they blamed his youth. Chastened, they turned the car around, went shopping and enjoyed their meal.

By the time they returned to his house, three hours later, the guard said Chris still was not there. The man working the gate clearly was embarrassed and felt terrible for my parents, but he had a job to do. He gave them the bad news and again asked them to wait a few minutes so he could contact Chris again. He returned to tell Hilda and Ed that Chris had changed his mind and would allow them on the grounds.

Upon entering his home, my parents were shocked to learn that Chris had a housekeeper. They thought one reason Chris might have been hesitant to have them wait for him there was because his place was a typical single guy pigsty – or at the very least, not clean enough for the fastidious Mrs. Hilda Martin. Such was not the case. His house was nearly immaculate.

About thirty minutes later, Chris arrived.

My mother described the next two days as one of the most humiliating experience of her life. Webber made it obvious they weren't wanted. She held her tongue while Ed tried to make the awkward situation seem normal. The last thing he wanted to hear from his wife was, "I told you so." Possibly for the first time, Ed began to see that this Chris Webber with money in his pocket was not like the young Chris who asked Ed to increase the support for him and his family as their benefactor.

The first day of the California trip made Mom bitterly aware that Webber would do as little as he could to honor his commitment to her husband. Meanwhile, Ed, with all the dignity and self-respect he could muster, wrangled a confirmation from Webber that they could spend the night. Mom said she agreed only because she could tell that her husband wanted desperately for the visit to succeed. But if the vibe was the same in the morning, she would tell Ed that their visit had to be shortened.

She didn't sleep well. She said she just couldn't stop thinking,

"Here I am, in the home of a kid who has done everything at my house. Our door was always open to this boy and his family. And now he treats us like this. It breaks my heart."

The next morning they arose to see little had changed. Some members of Chris' entourage had arrived and as I talked on the phone with Mom it was difficult to hear her over the background noise. I heard enough to get the gist of the situation.

Nothing changed over the rest of the trip. While Dad tried to pretend Webber wanted them there, Mom was disgraced.

Chris Webber and Hilda Martin

My parents had not just "dropped in" on Chris with that visit. It was planned and coordinated and inked in on his calendar long before. Their host allocated no time to be with guests who had been like his extended family, who had travelled so far to celebrate a major moment with him, and who had done so much for him. That was bad enough. What was worse was that it seemed as if he was deliberately trying to make them feel unwelcome. In that he succeeded.

There are moments that reveal the character of a person. This was such a moment. It was not the only one for me throughout my relationship with Chris Webber. But it was one of the lowest, one of the most gratuitously hurtful to my mom, a lady who had always been so giving and kind to him.

Dad and I often discussed what kind of talks Webber's parents had – or didn't have – over the years with their son. As much as Chris Webber's actions say about him, they speak volumes about his parents.

In a typical incident, after exhausting all other attempts to get straight answers, to conclude this business of Webber making good on his full obligations, one day my Dad and I took it to the office of Webber's attorney. We felt we had no choice other than to take this step because Webber had not answered our many telephone calls. So we made an appointment to hear what Webber would have to say.

We made small talk with the attorney, Fallasha Erwin, before Dad said calmly, "We are here to discuss the how and when of Chris paying us back."

Attorney Erwin did not seem at all surprised. To me that meant that at some point, the Webbers had told the lawyer that they had received money from Ed. Mayce Webber knew he had a substantial unpaid debt, and that one day there would have to be a collection call.

That in mind, the lawyer's response surprised us.

If the goal is just to have a conversation, he said, there is no need to call Chris. He never answers the phone and he rarely calls back. So let's don't waste our time dialing those ten digits. Instead, he suggested, let's call Deacon Mayce Webber – he usually answers or calls right back.

Erwin dialed. One ring. Two rings. Three rings. More. Finally, Deacon Mayce Webber answered.

Without speaking to the Deacon himself, Erwin passed Ed the phone.

"Hey, Deacon, how you doing?" Ed, at his most congenial. "It's been a while since we talked. Yeah."

Less than half a minute later, staring at the receiver in disbelief, my father hung up the phone. For that rare time in his life, the talkative Big Ed Martin was speechless.

As for me, I was baffled and wondered, "In just those few seconds, what does one man say to a long-time benefactor who has done so much for him, his son and his family to cause that kind of reaction?"

"He just told me to do him a favor," my father said, choking out the words, "and never contact him or his son again."

Yes, obviously we had been slow learners. No denying we had been too trusting. We should have known what to expect the moment Chris delivered the bag with $38,200. There couldn't have been any doubt after the way my parents were treated by Chris at his California estate. Those were bad times, but not until that moment in the lawyer's office did we see starkly the true character of Chris Webber and Deacon Mayce Webber.

"Never contact him or his son again," the words my father repeated hung in the air as the three of us sat there in silence.

Lawyer Erwin had nothing to offer beyond shaking his head and raising his hands in a gesture of "What're you going to do?"

Finally my stunned father found some words. And years later when I taped the interview with him for this book, he repeated as if in a stream of consciousness what he had said in Webber's lawyer's office.

> *His parents knew everything he was getting from me! I would never hide anything. I would take overcoats, topcoats, suits to the house... leave them for him.*
>
> *We went places. We went to the movies. I remember we went to see Denzel Washington and Spike Lee in* Mo' Better Blues... *Chris kept talking about the scene where Denzel Washington's character gets his lip messed up and can't play the trumpet anymore. He said if he got hurt and*

messed up, he couldn't play basketball and that would be the same thing, more or less. He had to be careful.

I got hotel rooms for him and his friends, for him and his girl... places like the Hyatt Regency and the Ritz-Carlton. One night after he was in college I got him a place in Dearborn, out on Michigan Avenue. Matter of fact, Jalen stayed there, too. But Jalen's mother always tried to make sure she paid me back if I did something for Jalen. She didn't have a lot of money, but she didn't want him getting in any trouble. If I did anything with Jalen, she gave me the money back! That way, he'd be safe.

Big Ed Martin, Uncle Ed, my father... the bigger-than-life person who was so many things to so many people was now simply a deflated booster, a humiliated man. How many times had he gone over this litany of losses in his head since that phone call in the lawyer's office cut his legs out from under him? To him, what he had done for Chris Webber, what he had been to Chris Webber was so much more than just the money.

Oh, it's so many things I did for Chris! When his girlfriend was in Canada, I bought her flowers and different stuff. When he didn't have his girlfriend to take to the prom, I called her and got her to go to the prom with him. He's supposed to be this big-time athlete, and she didn't want to go! Eventually, she changed her mind.

When he was going to make his announcement about college, he really wanted to have a party. And I wanted him to have it, too. I wanted Chris to have everything he could have... So I was in charge of getting everything and setting up everything. I even went and bought the Michigan cap he put on when he made his announcement.

We went down to the 1940 Chop House in Detroit and set up a party... It was supposed to cost $1,600... ended up being almost $2,000... The pastor went, his whole team *went, people from Country Day... everybody he could have known, he invited them! Then there was another, smaller party at the Renaissance Center. I paid for that, too. That was for him and Jalen.*

However many times Ed Martin rehearsed the Webber script in his mind or said it aloud to me, he always ended up at the same place – at the final punctuation point in Chris Webber's betrayal that so devastated him.

I thought that he loved me, and that one day he was gonna take care of everything. He told me, 'You don't have to worry about nothin'.' He said he was gonna take care of it, you know?

CHAPTER TEN

Inside the Fab Five

Time may heal wounds but it has not diminished the notoriety of the University of Michigan's Fab Five. The aura surrounding that legendary quintet eclipses the individual members of college basketball's most famous recruiting class.

Even casual sports fans know the CliffNotes version: When five high school All-American superstars join forces in Ann Arbor, Michigan, they become the richest freshman haul in NCAA hoops history.

The quintet:

Ray Jackson, the quiet-but-deadly Texas shooting guard seemingly content to ply his game in the shadow of his better-known teammates.

Juwan Howard, the easy-striding, 6-foot-10 Chicagoan as capable of high-octane offense in the low post as he was of straightjacket-style defense.

Jimmy King, gap-toothed, quick-tempered, a guard/small forward possessed of a superhuman vertical leap and an appetite for a defender to posterize.

Jalen Rose, the charismatic point guard whose defensive relentlessness and fearless offensive forays into the lane embodied a 'hood-hardened style forged as much from Perry Watson's torturous practices as from Detroit's rugged streets.

Chris Webber, the 6-foot-10, 245-pound center/power forward, the Hall of Famer in-waiting, a middle-class man-child whose size, athleticism and intellect coalesced to turn him into arguably the single best college basketball player of his time.

These five young, African-American, hip-hop-flavored freshmen were unleashed on an unsuspecting basketball world. They would leave the game drastically different from the way they found it.

As a quintet, they were together only two years, but that was all the time they needed to refashion the college hoops landscape. The products of big-city blacktops from throughout the Midwest and Southwest, they injected a decidedly black and urban flavor to the game. They featured trash talk, dramatic hand gestures and gleaming bald heads and put it on display in a Midwestern university campus that prided itself on tradition with more than a touch of elitism.

By becoming NCAA championship finalists as both freshmen and sophomores, the Fab Five obliterated the age-old basketball gospel that a team can't win with five newcomer starters. And with their baggy shorts and black socks, they revolutionized basketball's dress code. Overnight they reduced snug, nut-hugging uniforms to laughable fashion relics.

Of course, the college basketball world had been transformed into a multi-billion-dollar cash machine long before King, Rose, Jackson, Webber and Howard ever took to a court together. Nevertheless, the impact of the prized quintet penetrated deep into the NCAA's bottom line. It took merely one game for the collegiate sports industry to recognize just how lucrative the Fab Five could become.

Driven by the national obsession of postseason "March Madness," the NCAA's basketball revenue had been climbing steadily in the years prior to the Fab Five's arrival. By the time Chris and Co. played their first game, the money generated by collegiate basketball had exploded beyond what anyone could have anticipated.

The Fab Five's first year, 1991, also marked the beginning of a seven-year, $1-billion mega-deal between CBS and the NCAA that gave the network the rights to broadcast every game in the tournament. The agreement, announced in 1989, poured nearly $143 million a year into the NCAA's coffers – nearly triple the size of the previous contract. The NCAA's own magazine, *Champion*, described the deal as "stunning" and a "game-changer."

Just as significant was the fact that 1991 also marked the start of a new compensation system for tournament entrants that found each college or university earning more money for each postseason victory. By 1995, with college hoops now in the midst of a TV ratings explosion, the NCAA and CBS were negotiating a contract extension through the 2002 tournament that was worth $1.725 billion. That was followed by an 11-year, $6 billion deal.

But even as the NCAA, academic institutions, TV networks and apparel manufacturers were setting up to earn billions, the players – including the Fab Five – were learning a harsh lesson about who wasn't eligible for a cut of the windfall profits basketball was generating.

Everyone was getting a juicy slice of a big pie – everyone but the players.

Even as freshmen in 1991, they may have been young, but they were nothing if not street smart. Each of them knew what it was like to be coveted, to have seemingly mature adults swoon over them. Their rare gifts on the hardwood sparked outlandish promises even as their intimidating bald heads and black game socks took off in popularity. Jimmy King says the look was the Fab Five's nod to the Black Power sentiment that infused hip-hop culture during that period. Young but not naive, they understood well the attention, power and revenue their brand could generate. But they also were painfully aware of how the same NCAA system that used their talents to turn athletic directors and TV execs into millionaires ensured that they could never receive a dime of those riches.

It was into that atmosphere that Webber and Rose hit campus. By that time, Ed Martin's relationship with them and with Detroit prep basketball had changed significantly. The last few players who kept Ed tethered to Southwestern had left or would soon be gone. Howard Eisley went to Boston College in 1990. Voshon Lenard earned a scholarship to the University of Minnesota in 1991. That same year, Coach Watson left his throne atop the prep basketball world to join Steve Fisher's coaching staff. In just two years, Southwestern High School lost much of its standout talent, as well as bidding goodbye to Coach P. Watt, the architect behind the program's decade of dominance.

My father, too, was moving on. Although he always had maintained ties to other great players around metro Detroit and the state, his friendship with the Webbers represented the first time he'd ever devoted significant attention to a non-Southwestern player. And now that Detroit's greatest high-school basketball program ever was ending its run, Big Ed began to consider branching out.

The problem wasn't just that the run was over, though. For my dad and Coach Watson, the end of the Prospectors' era also signified the end of what once promised to be a lifelong friendship.

In his early days on the fringes of the program, my father had been content to care for the players Watson had already assembled. But that role had elevated considerably from delivering Gatorade and snacks and taking the team out for meals.

He had steadily taken a more active role in the life of certain players. He talked with them about the colleges they were considering, which coaches would do best by them, which teams seemed most suited to their styles of play. And it was there that Ed Martin ran afoul of Perry Watson.

No player's situation illustrated that clash better than Howard Eisley's. Following his stellar junior season in 1989, in which he helped lead Southwestern to yet another state finals appearance, Eisley became a coveted recruiting prospect. Teams across the country were reaching out to Watson for an opportunity to sign his point guard to a scholarship. However, Watson had close ties to the Kent State program and made it clear to Eisley that he thought the Ohio school would be best for him.

Eisley wasn't so sure. Kent State was a Mid-American Conference (MAC) school, and he felt certain he wouldn't get as much exposure as if he went to play ball in, say, the Big Ten, Atlantic Coast Conference or Pac-12. As one of three main cogs, along with Jalen Rose and Voshon Lenard, on the team that won Watson his first state title, Eisley felt he had the potential to showcase a much higher profile than the MAC could provide. Against his coach's wishes, he began considering other options.

Ed Martin encouraged Eisley to look further afield. Tony Jones, a former assistant coach to Watson at Southwestern, convinced a friend at Boston College that Howard was the point guard they needed. After watching him in one playoff game, the friend agreed.

Eisley was understandably conflicted over which school or conference would be his best option. He decided to discuss his dilemma one more time with Watson – and also with Ed Martin. When he asked Ed's advice, the answer was unequivocal. Go East, young man, where your odds of making it to the NBA will be far better.

While Watson wasn't thrilled with Eisley's decision, he ultimately accepted it and continued to counsel and support his former player, even after he went off to Boston. But that incident changed Watson's perception of my father.

Ed was still his friend and still a friend to the program. But Watson was now slightly wary of a man who was increasingly carving out an expanding role for himself. As long as Ed's influence was limited to the locker room or the bleachers, all was fine. But this excursion into recruiting and player development drove a wedge and the two began to grow apart.

Years earlier, Ed had made it clear to Watson that he was backing Webber, even at Country Day. Now, by giving counsel to Eisley, for the first time, Ed's loyalties were divided. Clearly, his ambitions were much bigger than the Southwestern program. He had already shown in his support of Chris Webber that Big Ed Martin could take his money and his support anywhere he wanted. By attaching himself to Webber's star, he left no doubt he was more than willing to do just that.

The decision was unspoken: Ed wasn't abandoning Southwestern, but he had chosen his relationship with Webber over maintaining warm ties with Watson. Although Ed continued to hover around the Prospectors' program during Watson's final year there, it was apparent to me – even if it wasn't to the players – that P. Watt and Uncle Ed Martin were no longer the friends they'd once been.

The bond snapped totally and irreparably when Watson decided to leave Southwestern to join Rose and Webber at U-M. He had been cool with what Ed had done as long as it helped his Prospectors' program. Now that he was going to Michigan, Watson seemed to have decided he couldn't afford to be associated with Ed because he knew he couldn't control Ed's expenditures. A man who had aspirations of being a head coach at a major college couldn't risk the taint of an NCAA scandal. So the legendary high school coach stopped talking to Big Ed Martin.

For his part, my father still cared about Watson. That was not unusual because he didn't walk away without good cause from a relationship. But he realized that Watson wanted to distance himself from him and he understood why.

My mom had a different opinion of Perry, but then, she had always been leery of many of the people my dad was close to. She saw Perry as one of the many who took advantage of her husband. Mom would constantly remind Dad about all he did for Watson while the coach never did anything in return.

Ed would shrug it off. Watson was a Detroit public school teacher and basketball coach. Of course he didn't have a lot of money.

Hilda Martin didn't see it that way. She felt Watson didn't even show appreciation. "It doesn't cost much to prepare somebody a chicken dinner," she used to say.

Even though Watson was now at Michigan, Ed didn't need his friendship to operate there. He already was close to those at U-M who were most important: the players. The way he put it:

Sometimes I gave gifts to parents: cologne, cakes, a few dollars here or there, something like that. I gave a cake to Roy Marble when I went to Flint. And Terence Green, when he was a big star up at Flint, I left him a sweater. Marble, I bought him a sweater, too. Well, that wasn't for Southwestern. That was helping Michigan out. I was trying to recruit for them, but his father decided he didn't want Michigan to take him.

But I would give, and they knew that I would give to anybody. To Callahan's mother and father, to Hunt's mother and father, I took them stuff all the time. Perry's mother and father, I took them dinner, I used to buy fifteen dinners and take them to the whole basketball team. I bought stuff for Chris, Jalen, other people. I had all kind of stuff made. And they were happy. It was just something I did for kids.

Watson, Rose and Webber had taken a leap to the next level. And so had Big Ed Martin.

His "godson" was now the star attraction for one of the nation's most storied universities. Chris Webber and Jalen Rose were the most can't-miss pro prospects Ed had ever seen. These two kids who had dominated middle-school ball as the Superfriends were now captivating the college hoops world. It was all but a sure thing they would cash in, big time.

No longer was Ed bound by Perry Watson and his strict rules. And with Rose and Webber ensconced at U-M, Ed could do as he pleased. Maybe he didn't see it that way at the time, but his insistence on maintaining a relationship with Webber after he had chosen Country Day over Southwestern had been Ed Martin's declaration of independence from Perry Watson and the Prospectors.

Dad would always harbor fond memories of the program and of the many youngsters he helped at Southwestern. Now he could "help out" talented players on an even grander scale. Operating in the college ranks gave him an opportunity to see his charges through not just the formative years of high school and college but on to the big time, to the NBA.

Before Webber, Rose, Eisley or Lenard, the closest Ed had come to seeing one of his kids make it big was Joubert and Wheeler. But they were performing only in overseas leagues. Now, Ed had ties to guys with more than just a measure of pro potential. Suddenly, he had gone from rubbing elbows after high school games with superstars to riding in the orbit of potential Hall of Fame greatness. Even before their images skyrocketed as the most visible members of the Fab Five, Rose and Webber were projected as sure-fire NBA lottery picks. Lenard was also enjoying a standout college career, as was Eisely, who left the year before. All were being hailed as potential high-round NBA draft picks.

Ed was self-aware enough to know he couldn't be an agent or financial manager. For all his math prowess, he was still only a factory electrician. That didn't stop him from entertaining dreams of the NBA glory "his boys" would achieve and musing about ways he could be involved.

Maybe he wouldn't be anything more than a personal advisor or a board member on one of the players' charities. Maybe he'd just be good old Uncle Ed, whose charity would be fondly recalled at holidays. Perhaps one of them would fund a scholarship in his name. Dad didn't care where his seat was in the inner circle of the future pros he helped nurture. He just wanted to belong.

With no P. Watt to rein him in, Ed grew bolder with his giving and spread his money around even wider.

When word got back to him that Voshon Lenard, then in his sophomore season at Minnesota, was struggling to brave the bitter Minneapolis winters without a heavy coat, Ed immediately had one shipped to Minneapolis. It was not some inconspicuous down jacket, but a full-length leather coat with a fur hood. Let the kid cut a figure.

The Webbers may have benefited the most from Ed's largesse, but they weren't the only ones associated with the Maize and Blue who received his help. Rose got more than a few dollars under the table – during his time at Southwestern and at Michigan.

"Ed helped them both out a lot, but Jalen was always cooler about his, always had other places he could turn to other than Ed," recalled Fred Lamar, a high-school friend of Rose's who later became an integral part of Webber's entourage during the Fab Five era. "Jalen had come out of Southwestern, so he knew how he was supposed to deal with Ed. He loved Ed just like the other Southwestern guys did, so with him there wasn't any trying to use Ed or trying to get over on him.

"Jalen went to Ed with what he needed. Ed would do anything for Jay or Chris, and he was always making sure they had a couple of dollars in their pockets. But Jalen always made sure that he only went to Ed when he didn't have any other choice. Chris was living off of Ed."

Though Webber and Rose maintained the closest ties to Ed, it didn't take long before Big Ed had won over every one of the Fab Five. Ed was nowhere near the benefactor to King, Jackson or Howard that he was to Rose and Webber, but he did his best to spread at least a little cash around the locker room. Even today, former teammates of Webber and Rose look back fondly on Ed.

"Ed was just a good person," King said. "When you come into the school, people from the area want to connect you with people who can help you and people that need to be a mentor or should be a mentor. We were meeting a whole bunch of people. I was meeting people in Ann Arbor, people out of Lansing, people in Detroit. I was meeting people everywhere, and he was a good guy to me.

"The first time I actually spent time with him was when we were in Ann Arbor. He invited us to his home. It was early in our freshman year, like in the fall, a couple of months into school. We had been on campus for a little bit. I think all five of us went down there and spent some time with him in his living room. We just sat there and just talked about life, about school, about what we wanted to do, what were our expectations. He was just kind of like, you know, 'I'm a friend. I am here to help you if you need any help'."

King said he knew Ed was tight with Webber and Rose, but it wouldn't be until years later that he realized just how close they were. King learned quickly that Ed was genuine in whatever he did or said. "He did it for kids," King said. "And that is why everybody I know, including myself, held him to a different standard. That was from his heart. That's who he was.

"In the first encounter we were just like OK, you know, this home is open to us if we ever need it, if we got caught in a bind or just need to talk, anything. He was there for us. That was it. Then I would see him occasionally at a game or around, or he would come see us. He wouldn't give a call, he would just show up. He'd say, 'I came to check on you. Are you alright?' That was it. 'Is everything cool? Are they treating you right?'

"I am still stuck on how people could say that he somehow took advantage of players. I do not understand how people can draw that conclusion about someone that helps all kids. And that's exactly who Ed was, a person who cared about kids. He did not look for kids' involvement to benefit him and the university he was aligned with. That's what real boosters do. They help their school or a particular program.

"When people say Ed was a booster, they're wrong. He helped everybody. A booster is only going to help a player if it benefits him and his university. It was not like that with Ed," King said. "He wanted to see if we were OK because he understood that we were in situations where we were at this major university and we could not use it. We were at this major university and we couldn't get around.

"The only thing I would like to emphasize is something most people who are not close don't understand," he said. "Ed had one of the purest hearts of anyone you will ever want to meet. He was a genuinely good guy. You know, people who got an angle, they always trying to get something out of you. That wasn't Ed at all. And that is something that I think people need to know, if they don't know."

King estimates Ed gave him no more than a total of two hundred dollars during his Fab Five career. King, who left Michigan after his junior season, said he never saw Ed dole out huge sums or exorbitant gifts to Webber or Rose, either, though he acknowledges that they could have been compensated without his knowledge.

"I know what the level was with me," King said. "With me, Ed's conversation was, 'Are you are all right?' And I had my pride, so I would always tell him, 'Yeah, I'm cool.' But he really knew I wasn't cool. He'd just be like, 'You know what? Don't even… this is for you. I know the situation that you're in.' He was real like that. He talked to my parents. My parents talked to him. We got to know him."

As he looked back, King sounded almost regretful that he and his teammates didn't get more of a chance to cash in.

"At Michigan, I am sure boosters exist," he said. "I know they exist. But I did not have any. That was why me and some of my teammates were pooling our money together. We were looking around like, 'We're just kind of out here.' That is what it was. I found out later that players from other universities seemed to be getting treated well except for us. North Carolina, Kansas, Kentucky. You know how it is in our basketball fraternity, right? The stories they used to tell me….

"I'm not shocked, because I know. But they used to laugh at me talking about how we'd get in trouble for accepting gifts. 'Get in trouble? What?' So it was known while we (the Fab Five) were there that we were under a microscope, a big microscope. And the school left us out there. So for people to talk bad about Ed is crazy. He was trying to help, not hurt anybody. And when you're hungry and broke and watching everybody else make money off you *but* you, I don't think it's wrong for a kid to get help. I think that's only fair."

These recollections are indelible for those who were directly involved in these events. Perhaps that shouldn't be surprising because some of these happenings were far out of the ordinary.

My father recalled the time a few of his young, street-toughened associates in the numbers rackets contacted him with a proposition that they handle some business regarding Chris Webber.

As his NBA career began to blossom, Webber would make frequent trips back to Detroit whenever his schedule permitted. These visits were ostensibly to see parents and family, but his motivation was primarily to hang out with his boys and bask in public adulation as The Returning Hero.

On one visit, a big bash was held at the State Theatre downtown for Webber and other pro players with Detroit pedigrees. It was billed as something like the "Return of the Big Ballers." It was an almost instant sellout. I was definitely going to attend, because I knew some of the promoters staging the event, and because it had become the talk of the town.

With all that hoopla, Ed eventually heard about it, too. So did some of his younger business associates who liked my father and had made considerable money working for him. Now they were willing to go to the wall on his behalf.

According to my father, one of them said, "Hey, Ed. Chris is in town. At least for one night, we know where he's going to be, and he's got to enter and leave the theater."

"I think I know where you're going with this," Ed replied, "but what's your point?"

"Well, has he paid you back yet?"

"No, he hasn't come correct yet."

"We didn't think so. Why don't we go down there and talk to him? Real personal-like."

Suddenly Ed realized what they were asking. They wanted to confront Webber outside the State Theatre and let him know it would be in his best interest to repay Ed as he had promised.

Now, they respected Ed; they wouldn't have taken Webber out on his behalf, but they definitely would have left their mark. One even suggested damaging a knee (or two) to put a crimp in his sky's-the-limit young career.

Ed's response was swift and sure. "I understand what you're asking, and I appreciate the offer. I really do. But I have to say no."

"Why not?" they protested.

"I can't hurt those boys, I just can't. They can hurt me, but I can't hurt them. It's not in me to do that."

Chris Webber – and possibly a few other players who were indebted to Ed – had no idea how close they came to having total strangers run up on them and wreak vengeance in his name. I suspect, given Dad's legendary generosity, some friends volunteered to do his debt collection as a freebie, knowing he probably would give them a share of whatever they recovered.

Yes, to Ed Martin's mind, the Webbers had abused his generosity. They had betrayed a cherished friendship. They had reneged on a solemn promise and failed to make good on a debt. Yet he could never cause or allow harm to come to them.

Somehow, despite his disappointments, he would not let himself become disillusioned. Deep in his heart, he believed that if he ever really needed assistance, his players would step up for him. Beginning with Antoine Joubert, then so many others, even including Chris Webber and the Fab Five. Sure, if needed, they'll be there for me.

He could not know how soon and how severely that faith would be tested.

CHAPTER ELEVEN

Piling Up Assists

There were two other U-M players similar to Chris Webber who developed a relationship with Ed Martin while they were in high school, asked for additional assistance, and didn't attend Southwestern: Robert Traylor and Maurice Taylor.

Ed met Robert "Tractor" Traylor in 1992 between his freshman and sophomore years at Murray Wright High School in Detroit. There was an immediate connection between Robert and my Dad and I am not sure why. I know many are thinking it's because Robert was a 6-foot-4 basketball phenom when he was 15 years old. Yes, it was that, but it was so much more.

The obvious answer is Ed was the father figure Robert never had. True, but not the whole answer. Before my Dad met Robert he had another man in his life that looked out for him and the Traylor family. His name is Larry. Larry was younger version of Ed Martin – great guy, great intentions, always putting the kid's concerns first, always providing more than just money.

I learned that Larry worked out with Robert for nearly four years. Over time, the growing connection between Robert and Ed made the Traylor family forget about Larry. Some may suggest this happened solely because Ed offered more assistance. Some may say it's because Ed was now well known in the basketball community for doing things real big.

At this time, Ed was supporting Chris Webber and Jalen Rose

who were in the midst of leading the University of Michigan team to two Final Fours. Voshon Lenard just finished his freshman season at University of Minnesota averaging close to 10 points per game. Howard Eisley was doing very big things as a sophomore at Boston College. Maurice De Shawn Taylor was a year away from being in the family and was a Top-50 recruit out of Henry Ford High School in Detroit.

The connection that grew between Ed and "Tractor" was like the easy comfort you see between a grandfather and a grandson.

Robert was raised by two women: his grandmother Jessie Carter and his Aunt Lydia. Carter was the provider, protector and damn near everything else for Robert, raising him when her daughter could not.

One thing I have learned is that the influence all parents have on their kids is powerful. Whether we consciously choose to accept it or not it tends to weave itself into our DNA. I was first made aware of this fact by a local Nike rep who covered the high-school basketball scene for as long as Ed had made high-school kids apart of his life. He was the first to ever know that most of the kids Ed helped did not show appreciation afterwards for that assistance. I asked him how he knew? He replied, "Character is learned at the knee." And most people who have a child that may someday be an NBA player have not disciplined that child appropriately.

In that regard, Carter was an outlier. She never let Robert get away with anything because he was destined for the NBA. Whenever he slipped up, she gave him an earful. One thing I noticed in the Traylor household that didn't exist in other homes, was that Carter was always the parent. Regardless of how much money Robert made, their relationship never changed. Grandma Carter was a strong woman with a powerful sense of right and wrong that she herself lived and that she preached to her grandson.

Traylor's second mother was his Aunt Lydia, she was as sweet as she was physically dominating. She stood 6-foot-2 and had

Robert "Tractor" Traylor cut an imposing figure, whether on the court or dressed to impress at a social event

played basketball on a Division-1 scholarship at University of Detroit Mercy. In more ways than one, she laid the foundation for her nephew's game.

When Lydia sat down to be interviewed for this book, the first time she spoke the name Ed Martin, she paused to compose herself and wipe away tears. We consoled each other as we silently realized how much loss we had endured over twenty years: Grandma Carter, Ed and Robert.

Around the Martin house, we had always referred to the Traylor home as the "land of the giants." Imagine six people, four of them over 6 feet tall and over 225 pounds living in a three-bedroom, one bath, 1,100 square-foot bungalow on Detroit's West Side. I can still remember the laughs I shared with FBI agent Jim Tritt when he told me about his visit to the Traylor home.

Although nobody in the Traylor or Martin family was Catholic, most Fridays Ed sat down with the Traylors for a fish dinner. Aunt Lydia, head swaying side to side and talking through a sly smile, said she looked forward to Ed showing up with some fish and a bottle. Sometimes Ed brought in carry-out. Sometimes the Traylors prepared the fish dinner in their kitchen. On beautiful summer days, they grilled outside. Whether the main course was salmon, tilapia, perch, catfish or some new fish delicacy, these people sat down together and enjoyed a meal once a week for more than six years.

The tradition continued after Tractor went to Michigan. When Ed Martin entered a family's life, he became a family member.

That's why when Tractor had to decide where to play college ball, Ed's input was as meaningful as Aunt Lydia's. People always assume that Ed's assistance bought him proximity and influence. Although the assistance helped, the closeness came when they learned Ed truly cared. One such time came in 1997, while Tractor was a student and basketball player at U-M.

The FBI had previously received federal subpoenas to tap our telephone calls. Then, one taped conversation changed the direction of their investigation. According to Ed, a troubled Traylor called Ed one evening from his U-M apartment. Traylor said he was tired, that the university wanted too much from him. He described having to attend a booster function after practice and that he had homework to do. But if he didn't attend, he could lose his scholarship.

Ed told the worried Traylor he doubted they would revoke his scholarship. Ed advised him to be honest, to tell U-M he can't do everything and, if necessary, he could take his game to Wisconsin where he would come back and kick Michigan's ass.

Traylor said he couldn't transfer anywhere without sitting out a season. Ed, who knew the NCAA rules, said Tractor could transfer if he didn't take a scholarship, and Ed would pay his way elsewhere, if necessary. Armed with that financial assurance, Traylor put aside his concerns.

That's what Ed wanted to provide for all his guys: let them

Already well known as a high school phenom, Robert "Tractor" Traylor was no diamond in the rough, but he already had an appetite for bling, with Uncle Ed Martin handling the tab

know they weren't alone; that they had options as long as he was breathing. He wanted to shield them from life's distractions, to assure them that if their family needed help, if they needed pocket change, he would help.

Being young and having to be the man of the house is a reality in many inner-city homes. Ed reminded Traylor that now the job he had to do was to play ball, focus on academics, and keep his nose clean. Ed made it clear that he would take care of the rest.

On another phone call recorded by the FBI, Traylor told my dad that he'd been approached by guys wanting him to fix a game or two. Ed told him in no-uncertain terms to never talk to them again.

Ed wasn't raided because he ran an illegal gaming business. He was raided because he gave to athletes *and* ran an illegal gaming business. If Ed never gave a penny to any athletes the FBI would have never pursued their investigation of him. In fact, FBI Agent

Greg Stakal told me that as early as 1982 they were aware of Ed's numbers business.

Ed Martin was raided for one reason only: because the FBI believed he was using his influence with the players to fix games.

Yet, according to the FBI and IRS agents involved, they looked at the score of every game of players connected with Ed and found absolutely no evidence of fixing. This conversation between Ed and Robert was completely in line with their analyses of the betting line and final box scores.

Something else we learned about another phone call came from Lydia. When Traylor got his first NBA check, he called home. He asked his grandmother if they were going to take care of Ed. Grandma Carter's reply was they were going to repay Ed before doing anything else, that Ed would be the first person he paid with every check.

I can never express how much that meant to my father – to feel that warm glow of someone doing the right thing.

From his first check until he paid Ed back in full, Traylor never missed a payment. He paid my father $5,000 out of every NBA check. He continued making the payments even after Ed was raided. We only wish the other players had the same integrity and honor as the Traylor family.

Ed Martin had given more than $600,000 to Robert "Tractor" Traylor, Chris Webber and Maurice "Mo" Taylor. These three were the only three players who requested additional assistance and agreed to pay it back. Collectively, that trio earned more than $242 million from their pro basketball contracts alone. Their endorsement deals undoubtedly totaled millions more. To date, all of them have repaid a total of $148,200. Of that, $110,000 came from Traylor.

Just after Christmas of 1991, Dimitri Sandifer, a good friend of mine, had stopped by the house and told me there was a sophomore kid at Henry Ford High who had game. Back then, as a 28-year old with my own business, my holiday season was rather easy and I actually had some time so I decided to go see this Maurice "Mo" Taylor, check out his game.

I left the house curious but doubtful. I mean, come on, Henry Ford High hadn't produced a real baller since Greg Kelser. Never did I think the kid I was about to see could be as good as he turned out to be.

Right away, I was impressed. There was no doubt in my mind that this young man was a next level player. He was raw – and I could scarcely believe this – it was only his second season playing organized basketball. I was interested.

Following the game, I gave the nod to my guy, Dimitri, meaning I'd like to meet him even though I was skeptical about becoming his mentor-handler or giving him a boatload of money. Dimitri and I walked down the bleachers to the gym floor and he motioned for Taylor to come over.

I found him to be a pleasant young man who was well-rounded and presented himself admirably for his age. He had an adequate knowledge of the game, especially considering the short time he had been playing.

As I left the gym, I thought this is my chance to show my father I had his eye for talent. Already I wondered if Maurice De Shawn Taylor would go Big Ten, ACC or Pac-10. I was certain this talented, 6-foot-9 athlete would be playing far beyond Henry Ford. If he developed, he had an excellent chance to make the NBA.

I went to see Taylor play in his next game and Henry Ford recorded another win. Because it was our second conversation, everyone felt more comfortable about the potential of me becoming Taylor's benefactor.

Following Ed's playbook, I planned our next meeting to include Taylor's parents. I was not going to have a relationship with a 16-year-old without ensuring his parents were aware of who I was and what my intentions were.

Two days later, I called Taylor after he got home from school to see if I could stop by his home and chat. He readily agreed and gave me his address. I showed up at the appointed time only to find that the adult there was not his parent. I later learned that his mother lived in Tennessee and his father was in Michigan, but was not heavily involved in his life. I can't recall who the man was at this first meeting. What I do know is that Taylor's Aunt Sabrina was raising him. The first adult I met gave approval for my involvement, which included mentoring Taylor in many aspects of life.

I later learned that Taylor had me meet him at that house in the Henry Ford school district because he wasn't sure his aunt would be open to receiving assistance. She would not put herself in a situation that would allow anyone to question her ability to raise him.

In 1992, I was a real estate salesperson and my wife Robin and I owned a real estate company. We did well as far as providing for our needs, but we didn't have a lot of discretionary money. Still, I sponsored Mo through the end of his junior season. He came by my house so often during the summer after his junior year that our entire neighborhood knew who the tall guy was – or at least, who he was coming to see. In time, more people than we ever imagined would know about Taylor and his frequent visits to Orleans Street.

In the beginning, I was home most of the time. Taylor and I would have conversations that I would characterize as life coaching and he would leave with cash in hand. Eventually, my son knew why Taylor was stopping by. Anytime I wasn't home, Robin and Brandon knew that a white envelope for him was on the mantelpiece in the living room. So, here I was, Ed Martin Jr., offering assistance to another black kid loaded with athletic potential.

Taylor's junior season started out with a big splash. He had improved his play to the point where it was obvious to everyone that he was a top-tier Division-1 player. He had room to grow, but his footwork, shooting touch and feel for the game had advanced tremendously from his sophomore year. It's amazing how it happens: the more they show, the more you are willing to give. This was probably the time when the $100 weekly envelope grew to $200, plus a little something extra for expenses.

As the state basketball playoffs approached that season, Taylor said he wanted a gold chain. Well, why not – he did have an outstanding year and he seemed to be developing into a fine young man. A few days later we went to Southfield's Advance building, where everyone in the metro area with an ounce of 'hood went to get their gold.

The gold chain purchase changed everything. The purchase we made that day satisfied Taylor exactly 45 days. On day 46, he wanted something bigger. Anything bigger was out of the question, because it was out of my budget.

My only option now was to introduce Taylor to Big Ed himself. I added it all up one day and found that over an 18-month span I had given Taylor $20,000 in cash and gifts. For a high-school sophomore or junior, $250 or so a week is a ton of cheddar. Without having realized it, despite my limited means at the time, I had been giving excessively to a teen-age basketball player. Like father, like son.

Over that year and a half, my father and I had several conversations about Taylor, discussing the good and the not-so good. Now, however, I had to ask him a question to take over Mo Taylor's assistance program, because the expense was too rich for my budget.

"Son," he said, "since you are asking me this question I know this is what you would like to happen. And because you are my son, my answer is yes."

With Dad willing to pick up the player I'd begun mentoring and assisting, we picked a day and time to have Mo pay a visit so I could make the introduction.

One sunny day in May of 1993, Taylor rolled up onto Ed's driveway.

When he entered the house, it was as if he already had his hand extended. After brief pleasantries and small talk, Ed focused the conversation. He knew Taylor wanted a substantial boost in his assistance, so abruptly, he came right out and asked Taylor if that was correct.

Taylor said all the right things. He had supreme confidence that his talent was the trump card in this game. Recalling Mo's words years later, knowing what happened, what he said rings hollow. He expressed several times that he would take care of Ed as soon as he turned pro. The only thing left for Ed to do was to meet Taylor's parents, or in this case, his guardian.

Ed met Sabrina at her bungalow on Detroit's West Side, on Evergreen near Fenkell. As big a fan as Ed was of what Taylor could do on the court, he was even more impressed with his Aunt Sabrina. Sabrina, who was his mother's sister, had stepped in to raise her nephew when his parents couldn't. She was kind, gentle and definitely made Mo the priority in her life.

Soon Sabrina became one of Ed's favorites and regularly benefitted from his generosity. The more time she spent with Ed, the more comfortable she became. After a while, everyone got on the same page. Ed had so much respect and admiration for Sabrina that I believe if she hadn't been his guardian, the relationship between Taylor and Ed would have ended while he was at U-M.

This was the summer before Taylor's high school senior season. He and Ed had become fully connected and Taylor was ready to roll. Ed welcomed his newest protégé with one of his famous handshakes known as 'the money grip' and a trip to the stores where he could now shop with prior approval from Big Ed.

I was still involved with Mo on some levels. I tutored him as a senior when it came time for him to take his ACT test, even recruited a friend of mine, Othell Little, to assist him in math as we attempted to make him focus on the mechanics of taking a test. But for the next four years (as a high-school senior and his freshman, sophomore and junior years at U-M) Ed was the main man when it came to taking care of Taylor, and occasionally Sabrina, when they needed help or wanted to splurge. Mo Taylor wanted what he wanted when he wanted it, and showed no shame in asking for it. Or in accepting it.

How much "help" did Ed Martin bestow on Mo Taylor? When the FBI raided Ed's place, they found tallies, notes and receipts totaling $110,000 related to Taylor. That translates to four years of Dad giving Taylor an average of $528 per week. Now, anybody with a grain of sense knows that no high-school or college kid needs that much allowance. There are grown men providing for a wife and children that don't pull down that much every week. But when Ed was committed, Ed was excessive.

Just as Ed Martin and Chris Webber were a terrible combination, so were Ed and Mo Taylor. A gifted kid with a sense of entitlement and no boundaries when it came to asking for money, matched with a deep-pocketed, obsessive benefactor? Most times this doesn't end well.

Ed and Taylor's relationship was unique.

Taylor was 17 when he met Ed. Most 17-year-old high school seniors are far less impressionable than younger teen boys. Every other player Ed supported, he initially spotted when the kid was in eighth, ninth, or at the latest the tenth grade. A young man is far more open and willing to hear what an older benefactor is telling him at 14 than he is at 17.

There is no substitute for time. The effusive manner in which Southwestern players speak about Ed is indicative of their environment, yes, but also of the considerable time Ed spent with them.

On reflection, I've been able to see more clearly why Taylor's relationship with Ed was not as tight as they might have wished. My Dad was already steeped in a positive relationship with "Tractor" Traylor when I took Mo to meet him. I am certain that Ed's closeness to Tractor had an impact on Taylor. He may have felt like the stepson while Tractor was more like Ed's kid.

Perhaps for Taylor, this relationship was a positive one only from a financial perspective. It may be that being the player least connected to Ed on a personal level was a painful reminder for Taylor of his childhood. Growing up with no connection to one's parents can lead to many ugly, negative behaviors later on. That may explain what troubled Taylor. It may shed light on why, years later, he attempted what he did.

CHAPTER TWELVE

Crunching the Numbers

The world changed big time on February 17, 1996. A freak rollover accident triggered a series of shock waves that would ultimately reverberate through two major university basketball programs and the NCAA. That episode and the events it set in motion changed the lives of many players. For sure, life for the Martin family would never be the same again.

At five in the morning, a Ford Explorer careened off a slippery road seven miles east of Ann Arbor. In that vehicle were five U-M players, including four starters, and also a blue-chip MSU recruit. They were returning from a party in Detroit. The U-M players were Mo Taylor, Robert "Tractor" Traylor, Ron Oliver, Willie Mitchell and Louis Bullock. With them was Mateen Cleaves, a much-coveted player out of Flint Northern making a recruiting visit to U-M, obviously in a round-about route. Traylor suffered a broken arm and was lost for the season. Other U-M players were banged up but not seriously injured.

One result of the rollover accident was that Cleaves (who would go on to become the MVP of the NCAA 2000 Final Four) decided to avoid the intense media spotlight on U-M in the aftermath of the accident and take his talents to MSU. Big Ed Martin had met with Cleaves and his family while Cleaves was starring at Flint Northern. My father had good reason to be confident that if that highly publicized incident had never happened, Cleaves would have attended U-M. There, he would have teamed with Maurice Taylor, Tractor Traylor and Louis Bullock. That potent lineup would have instantly vaulted the Wolverines to elite basketball status. Hard to see how Cleaves would have fared better personally – he did well enough by melding seamlessly at MSU with Charlie Bell, Mo Peterson and other "Flintstones" to win the 2000 NCAA Championship.

While that event would eventually have dire consequences for my father and me, the beginning of 1996 was not all bad for the Martin family. On May 4, I got married and was about to start a family. I knew I needed to generate additional income. Up until this time, I was living comfortably as a single brother. My real estate business was humming along. I was learning the game from my mother-in-law and had bought and sold a few homes at a small profit.

All in all, I was doing okay. But doing only a bit more than getting by wasn't good enough. I decided I needed to increase income and the most obvious way to do that was to step up my involvement in the numbers business. I decided I would become a 'house' myself.

I knew my father would help me. Over the years, many people have asked if I was jealous or envious over my dad's generosity to the players. I always said no because he was more thoughtful and generous with the family than he was with his friends, associates or the players.

When I told my Dad I wanted to jump into the business with both feet, he was hesitant but didn't try to dissuade me. If I was going to do this, I had to take a responsible approach. Was I mature and disciplined enough for such a huge responsibility? Would I put the systems in place to ensure that everyone turned their numbers in on time? There were many details to get on top of.

Dad reminded me that I couldn't let myself be taken advantage of by someone trying to sneak an illegitimate bet past me. Some-

THE UNIVERSITY OF MICHIGAN
ATHLETIC DEPARTMENT

Joe Roberson, *Director of Athletics*

January 20, 1997

Mr. Edward L. Martin
17430 Fairway Dr.
Detroit, MI 48221

Dear Mr. Martin:

The University of Michigan has made numerous attempts to arrange an interview with you regarding your relationship with several of our student-athletes. These attempts include a telephone conversation with me and a similar conversation with Big Ten Conference representative, Robert Vowels. Our attempts also include a registered letter on October 30, 1996 requesting that you submit to an interview. As of this date you have not responded to my letter.

Your cooperation is critical to answering allegations of NCAA rule violations brought to the University by the NCAA. Your refusal to submit to an interview with University of Michigan and Big Ten Conference officials may jeopardize the eligibility of several of our student-athletes and may reflect negatively upon the University of Michigan basketball program as well. Without your response to several allegations, the University and the student-athletes are in a vulnerable position with relation to these allegations.

Once again, the University of Michigan and Big Ten Conference request that you submit to an interview as soon as possible. The University of Michigan and the Big Ten Conference do not object to your legal counsel being present during the interview.

I can not impress upon you enough the importance of your interview to the University of Michigan and our student-athletes.

Please notify me as soon as possible as to whether or not you will cooperate with our inquiry and submit to an interview.

Sincerely,

Joe Roberson

1000 South State Street   Ann Arbor, Michigan 48109-2201   Phone: (313) 764-9416   FAX: (313) 747-2754

My father and I were far from the only ones dealing with aftermath of the infamous rollover accident. The University of Michigan and the NCAA had questions to ask and questions to answer

thing like that could result in a $25,000 payout. Yeah, every once in while someone would hit a number on me – that was part of the business. But no one could sustain big losses from cheaters. Bottom line – I had to respect the rigors of the business if I were to run it properly.

He stressed that I had to be prepared to watch even my most trusted people because circumstances change in people's lives and sometimes so do their behaviors. Say that John, one of your runners, gets word that his mother needs an operation to live. If John has no financial means to pay for her care, his normal trustworthiness may change. He sees the amount of money you're taking in each week and his mind starts to work. He tells himself that he is not stealing, just doing what he has to do to care for his mother and after all, it's not like this is legal money earned through work, so what's the problem?

Dad also reminded me of what many people regard as the biggest drawback to the numbers business: you are tied to it six days a week year-round. Even when the plant shuts down for its annual breaks, the street number business never stops. There is always the risk that a house can lose business if it takes a week or two off.

That all made sense. But how do I get started? What's the first step?

Dad and I talked that over a while before we decided that I should team up someone already in the game. We had a trusted family friend named Waistline and I could become his house while he schooled me on the ins and outs of the street number business. Waistline thought that made sense all the way around, so he left the house he was previously working with and started steering his business to me. Before long, I could see there were nuances to the street numbers business. Waistline could teach me the subtleties that made working numbers on the streets different from the plant numbers business. Teaming with a street-savvy guy like Waistline was the best way for me to apprentice.

I started with two distinct advantages. First, my father loaned me $50,000 to be the house. Second, his reputation and connections helped me through a smooth transition. Over the fifteen months that Waistline and I worked together, the business grew but we ran into a few conflicts with customers. Waistline and I took a different approach to conflict resolution so we mutually agreed to separate and each run our own operation. I was now in business for myself.

And a thriving business it was. Soon after going solo, my 'high' for the week was $120,000. The high is basically the total amount of money (bets) that the runners and unit men turn into the house. In a traditional business environment, this is called the gross revenue. The 'low' is the gross income minus the expenses related to gathering the bets. The profit is what remains after deducting the expenses and paying the hits (winning plays).

If the house is the brains and the heart of a numbers business, the runners are the legs and the face. They're the ones who come face-to-face with the customers, take the bets from the individual players and collect the money. Typically, they receive 25 cents on every dollar they collect. So if they collect $100 worth of bets, they turn in $75 to the unit man. Unit men usually manage the runners for the larger houses and receive 5-10% of what they manage.

The math was simple: a high, or gross, of $120K a week comes to $6.24 million annually. True, that would be considered a decent little numbers business, but I knew that with my connections and my reach, I could make it blossom even more. Confident as I was, it was a pleasant surprise when my business grew faster than I had expected.

Now my big worry was whether I could handle the expanding volume. Along with the additional business came a growing concern whether I could pay off all the hits if a popular number were to fall. That worry is part of the business for a house and I knew that going in. So, I just accepted living with those fears and prayed that lady luck would be on my side. That had worked all those years for my dad so I figured it would work for me. As long as I could cover the hits, I knew that over time the house always wins. One more thing. I did have a unique security blanket because I knew Dad would be there to back me up if need be.

To give you an example of the exponential growth, about eighteen months later, my high for the week was $460,000. Annually that computes to $24 million in gross revenue. Of that amount, the house profits between 5-10% depending upon the expenses and volume of hits. So, when the weekly high was $120,000 that left me with about $6K per week and by the time the high hit $460,000 I was making about $23K per week. If that level sustained for a full year, that would yield almost $1,196,000. That was transforming for my family and me.

Now let there be no secret that the best thing about the numbers business, without question, was the constant flow of cash passing through my hands. I was then age 35, and it was an incredible feeling to have $20,000 at my disposal at any moment. Every day, as I was out on my routine circuits, my left pocket held $2,000 while stashed in my right pocket was $8,000 so I could pay any small hits on the spot.

That in itself would be a remarkable life for a 35-year-old man. But there's more.

To run my business I kept $80K in my safe at home. That meant that during this time of being the house in my numbers business, I walked around every moment of life knowing that I had enough cash to purchase almost anything my heart could desire. It took discipline to stay focused and not succumb to the traditional temptations of a thirty-something guy.

Not to suggest I didn't do some careless and impulsive things when all that money was flowing in. One day my brother stopped by and enjoyed a meal with Robin and me. It was a gorgeous winter day when he arrived, but by the time he was ready to leave, the weather had turned nasty. The temperature dropped so much he would need to put on something warm just to make it home. So, Robin ran upstairs grabbed a sweatshirt out of my closet and handed it to Bruce. He pulled it over his head and as he started to leave, he thrust a hand into one of the pockets of the sweatshirt. He smiled as he pulled a wad of cash and asked, "Do you want this?"

He handed me the wad and I counted out twenty-five crisp $100 bills. Spontaneously I gave him five of those bills. Heck, I didn't even remember where that money came from. Sometimes during collections, I would grab a payment and shove it in a pocket, later forgetting the money was there. At that time in my life it made sense to stash $30,000 in various places in the house just for safekeeping. One such stash was in in my daughter's room. Robin and I had given our daughter one of those fancy dolls that never ever comes out the box, and one day I hid $8K inside the box with the doll, figuring it was an unlikely and safe place to stash some cash.

Carrying this much loot did have one obvious and very real drawback. Some people in the neighborhood of my unit men saw me stop by on a regular basis to pick up and deliver cash. One of my guys named Alan lived in a neighborhood that was slightly suspect. One day his niece alerted me that a few of Alan's neighbors might attempt to relieve me of some cash. So, the next time I went to his house I got out of the car with a very visible Glock .45 in my right hand. I give thanks that I never had to use that gun, never knowing if this foiled an actual robbery.

While I was pleased to make the money, it was a ton of work. I went from managing two units to twelve. Each of my unit men had ten to twenty runners with my biggest unit having more than forty runners. That one huge unit generated a weekly average of $100K each week with a one-time high of $160K.

In addition to what I was taking in from the business my runners developed at the plant, they collected numbers from the entire metro Detroit area. They covered all sorts of establishments – dry cleaners, barbershops, beauty salons, auto repair places, funeral homes, police and fire departments, courthouses, schools, and party stores. There were taverns like Al's Olympia Bar on Grand River in Detroit which had an area where patrons could play their numbers. There were social clubs, one of which was on Oakman Boulevard in Detroit. Name a spot, good chance we did business there.

It was a good ride, being the numbers man, being the house. The best moments of all were when I could give a few thousand dollars to my mother, something I did regularly then. Worth it all to see those shining eyes, that smile on her face.

I was happy the way my numbers business was growing, but I knew there was always more to learn. So I often went to Little Champs, the breakfast spot on Plymouth Road, where the older established numbers men hung out. I learned a lot from them about managing rapid growth. It was exciting, even though like any business it had its ups and downs.

I had about a dozen people stationed by phones to write down the numbers coming from the smaller runners crawling all over the city. The phone workers made anywhere from $300 to $800 per week. My most trusted and hardest-working right-hand man made $1,200. At its height my payroll for all of them was around $5,000 per week. There is no way to know how many people there were in all the numbers businesses in Detroit, but certainly many families were raised on the money circulating in the community, money that was generated by the numbers.

One key piece of equipment in the operation was the fax machine because it had a time stamp on it. I probably had twenty fax machines all over the city. The twelve writers monitoring phones would fax in their pages as well. I had three at my house, three more at my head guy's house and two more in my boy's loft in downtown Detroit. So, no one could ever use the excuse that the fax was busy or not available because they had at least three different places to send their business. It was vitally important to have all of the business in my possession before the number came out. That made it certain that no one could cheat you by claiming they had entered and paid for a number when they hadn't.

That ploy was tried on me only once.

There were relatively few people who traveled from business to business picking up their plays and then turning them into a unit man or a house. Frenchy was one of them. He had a habit of turning in his business just before 7:30 p.m, the single most crucial time in the numbers business because the winning number is televised at 7:29. On this particular day, Frenchy was running later than usual and called Byron to let him know he would be there shortly after 7:30. Byron agreed to take his numbers after checking with me. I told him to tell Frenchy that we will take his entries but with an asterisk.

When Frenchy turned in his business to Byron, he mentioned that he had a $30 straight three-digit hit and a $5 straight four-digit hit – both of these would have been the maximum plays for his book. Typically, plays like this were odd unless these numbers were well established by someone having played those exact numbers recently on his book.

When Byron called and described the details of what happened, I immediately felt that Frenchy was trying run a scam. I told Byron I would be there to look at his tickets to see if I could prove that Frenchy was trying to hustle us. An important job of the house was to serve as a detective and – if necessary – as muscle. The would-be charlatan has to see full face that his attempted deception has been caught. That's what keeps to a minimum the ensuing drama surrounding the exposure of a fake 'hit'.

But now we had to play it out, take it to wherever it had to go.

Frenchy told Byron that the $30 three-digit play came from a cleaners which was on the westside of Detroit. That was at the beginning of his route. He said the $5 four-digit play came from a barbershop on the east side of the city. That location was towards the end of his route. When I analyzed the tickets that he turned in late, after the 7:29 p.m. deadline, I noticed something that proved what French had done. The supposedly "winning" numbers were on consecutively-numbered tickets. In light of the timing and the locations, no way could those phony "winners" have been written consecutively.

I called Frenchy and asked him to meet me at a gas station.

When he jumped in my car he was stuttering a little more than normal. "Crazy," he said, "how both the big hits came out today."

"Yeah, Frenchy, that sure is crazy. It's also odd how both of these hits were max plays."

He was silent a moment, then said, "Well, that's how it happens sometimes."

I wondered what was going through Frenchy's mind. As for me, I was thinking that if someone tried to slip a smaller amount by me, I don't know if I would have caught it. But they get greedy, I guess, and go for max. Don't they know when you see a possible big payout like that, up go the red flags?

"Frenchy, Bryon told me that you said the $30 play came from the cleaners at the beginning of your route. Correct?"

He nodded.

"Byron also said you told him the $5 play came from the barbershop towards the end of your route. Is that right?"

"Correct."

I pulled out the two tickets with the would-be winning plays and I asked Frenchy how far it was from the cleaners to the barbershop. He said they were about 90 minutes apart by the time he goes in picks up the business at each location.

I pointed to the two tickets and said, "Frenchy, these tickets are consecutive. Number 3773 and number 3774. Yet, prior to today, the sequence of the numbers on your tickets have always matched the direction of your route."

At this point, Frenchy has to know I'm on to him. But he doesn't give up.

"Man," he says, "I was in the car when the number came out so there is no way I could have seen it on TV."

"Frenchy, I have been in this game way too long. We both know they report the number on the radio as well."

"I ain't trying to cheat you. You know I need for you to pay those hits otherwise my people are going to be after me and I don't have that kind of money."

"Frenchy, you better get out my car before I whup your ass. And take all of these numbers with you."

I never heard from him again.

Despite its ups and downs, as businesses go, the numbers business is a good one for everyone, especially the house.

The Frenchy Disconnection was a memorable episode in my numbers game career. It wasn't the only one.

One evening in 1997, I went to watch a basketball game at my high school alma mater, University of Detroit Jesuit High School. By then I had been in the numbers game for twenty-one months. To this day, I can almost feel that singular vibration when my cell phone rang, as if for whatever reason, that particular vibration was somehow different.

It was Alan, one of my unit men. First thing he said, "It's a massacre."

Powerful words. And ominous, coming from my most honest, organized, and trusted unit man.

"Okay, Alan. What does that mean? What happened?"

"A four-digit came out tonight," Alan said, "and I have about $30,000 worth of hits on the books."

If I recall correctly the date was something like 12-10-97 and the number that came out related to the date. I couldn't know then how much the total damage was going to be. Al had hits, so my other units were probably hit heavy as well. All I could hear ringing in my head was Al's, "It's a massacre."

I reassured Al with more confidence that I felt myself, something like, "Alan, don't worry. We'll take care of everything."

I hung up the phone and as I tried to turn attention back on the basketball game, my vision started to get blurry. I had no clue what was going on as those high school ballers raced up and down the court. All I could think about was this mounting pile of money I was going to be paying out. Like, how many of my other guys have this number on their book?

I couldn't leave until the game was over because my son was playing. It was agonizing watching the clock taking forever for time to expire so I could get out of there, get back home, get to my fax machine. Only then could I assess the grand total of the carnage. Massacre... that word kept ringing in my ear. Why are you getting so excited, I told myself over and over. It doesn't really have to be that bad. But I didn't believe what I was telling myself.

Good thing, because it was far worse.

Before I left for the game that night, I put each person's business in their respective folders so all I had on the fax when I returned were the totals for each one. I pulled the first one off and it reads $40,000, the next $30,000, the next one $100,000. In all, the total was $240,000 worth of hits in one day. It was truly a Massacre. I can remember it like it was yesterday. It was horrendous.

I did not have $240,000.

First thing I did, I talked to all my key guys. Then I began getting a handle on how much money I had and where I could find more. I knew I could count on Dad and I was right. He loaned me $50,000. With that help and what I pulled together everywhere else, I was able to cover $205,000 of the $240,000. Several of my other units had bills and so they covered the remaining $35,000.

In just a couple hours, I had plummeted way below broke.

As devastating as that day was, by the end of January 1998, only fifty days or so after Alan so correctly labeled the massacre, I had $80,000 back in my safe again. In essence, I cleared $130,000 from my business in that time frame – I had repaid my dad his $50,000 and still had $80,000 in reserve.

I had survived the largest swing of cash ever during my days in the number business.

A few months later, the most memorable day of my numbers career brought everything to a screeching halt.

CHAPTER THIRTEEN

The Raid: Full Court Press

It was not the beginning of the end. No, that would have to have been the rollover accident.

The end was announced on April 28, 1999, by Federal agents pounding on my front door.

BAM! BAM! BAM!

"Open the door!"

BAM! BAM! BAM!

Yeah, at that moment, at about 11 a.m., a Thursday in late April, it was over for us. The lifestyle, tranquility and sense of security my family and I enjoyed came crashing down around us.

And I absolutely did not see it coming.

BAM! BAM! BAM!

"Ma'am, open the door!"

When the end arrived, it didn't come in a hail of gunfire, the smashing of battering rams or the menacing drone of helicopters overhead. Instead, it had crept up on cat's paws – quietly, stealthily. The only prelude – which I never heard – was the silent drawing of weapons, the murmur of tense voices on our front lawn. Then, suddenly, without warning, it exploded with fists banging on the front door of my house and on many others across Detroit and beyond.

The unthinkable, the inconceivable, became shocking reality: a small army of ten federal agents rushed my home like ants swarming over a sugar cube. They invaded my quiet, tree-lined Stratford Street neighborhood wearing an alphabet soup of agency abbreviations on their bulletproof vests – FBI, IRS, ATF – and stormed through my front door as if they were hunting for Islamic terrorists.

And it wasn't just my house. At that same moment, organized, coordinated raids involving nearly a hundred agents were underway simultaneously at a dozen locations in Detroit and its suburbs. Big Ed Martin's key people were getting hit as well as mine. Dad's lavish four-bedroom home in the Detroit Golf Club community was the focal point, but because the feds mistakenly believed that he and I were in business together, my place was Target 1-A.

The staccato pounding of fists on our front doors announced the climactic scene in a drama stretching over many months of intensive federal investigation costing taxpayers millions of dollars. The cast include a multitude of attorneys, accountants, defendants, witnesses and government stooges.

When the government comes down on you, your initial reaction is that you must be the focal point for them, the centerpiece, the prime target. It sure felt that way at the time, but only later did I learn that I had it wrong. The Feds had deployed all that money, time and scrutiny to nail not me, but my father. They weren't after some small fry numbers operators, their target was the Super Booster – they wanted him badly. My wife Robin, my children and I were just collateral damage.

Jim Tritt, the lead FBI investigator in charge of the raids, told me years later that the largest home invasion squads – ten agents at my house, eleven at Ed's – were assigned to us. "We had done our research," he said.

Well, yes and no. Somehow their research hadn't illuminated them sufficiently that Dad and I were running separate operations. However, Tritt and Frank Scartozzi, the lead IRS investigator on our case, had done enough advance planning to make sure their best people were assigned to our two homes. And at the same moment their teams were mobilizing outside our houses, other units were preparing to burst through doors across southeast Michigan.

At every location, the same script played out: Frantic, insistent rapping... Urgent demands to "Open this door!"... Startled, anxious silence from within... Finally, acceptance of the inevitable, and the door would be unlocked, opened.

Different venues. One scenario.

In the 11000 block of Rutland Street on Detroit's West Side, agents rushed the home of Bennie "Preacher" Smith, one of my unit men.

Preacher's wife thought she had managed to conceal a white plastic bag stuffed with twenty-dollar bills and one-hundred-dollar bills. She had thrown her fur coat over the bag as it lay on the bed, then sat down on the coat. The ploy worked until the Feds asked Bennie if they had seized everything of value.

"As long as y'all got that white bag, I guess you do."

As the Feds looked at each other, Preacher's wife, sitting there in disbelief, screeched, "Preacher!"

Preacher's nickname was one of the more accurate ones—he had this tendency to talk too much. And his timing wasn't so good either.

A quick count revealed that white plastic bag contained more than $30,000. The agents had also discovered a bedroom safe filled with more than $670 in $1 bills.

On the city's East Side, in the 4000 block of Baldwin Street, agents invaded the first floor of a two-family flat belonging to my man Allen Hall, a runner for me. This is one way I eventually figured out how they had been following me. Allen was in his 70s and I often stopped at his crib for conversation as much as for business. Inside Allen's home they found three pistols, one of them loaded.

In a Detroit home owned by Albert Smith, investigators uncovered a bedroom safe containing $7,000. An additional $3,200 was stashed inside a briefcase in the kitchen nearby. This raid also turned up a paper shredder, two adding machines and two fax machines, all of which had become critical to my operation, and a pair of pistols.

About 35 miles south of Detroit, in the suburb of Monroe, at the Rutherford Boulevard home of Jessie Keesee, officials opened a safe containing $24,978. Keesee, who manned the production line at Ford's Dearborn facility, also was found to have more than $5,700 in his wallet and pockets. Agents impounded his 1999 Ford Explorer.

In suburban Southfield, just north of Detroit, the home of Cecilia Matthews turned up even more potentially disastrous evidence. Matthews, one of Ed's trusted runners, couldn't prevent federal agents from seizing tax documents, a coat in her bedroom containing $10,000 in cash, and a photo spread signed by Louis Bullock. One of the U-M players involved in the 1996 rollover accident, Bullock had gone on to play pro basketball in Europe.

One by one, house by house, the Feds were yanking building blocks out of the foundation of a gambling empire my father had taken thirty years to quietly, carefully construct. Although I had been in business for myself for only a little less than three years, they took me down right alongside him.

What we couldn't have known then was the amount of time, effort and scrutiny that assemblage of government agencies put into building their cases and nailing our asses. Ed Martin had been on their radar for more than two years, with Agent Tritt having inherited the case from the previous agent in charge.

Several months earlier, a relatively raw agent named Mark Davidson had initially opened the investigation after the "anonymous" call came into the Dearborn police who then contacted the FBI about Dad being the gambling kingpin of Ford Rouge. Before Davidson could fully delve into the allegations, he was transferred to the Bureau's office in neighboring Macomb County; Tritt took over the case in September of 1997.

Ed Martin was not Tritt's primary concern. At least, not right away. First, he had some real criminals to deal with.

"We were getting prepared for the trials of Jack Tocco, Tony Tocco, Tony Corrado, Paul Corrado and Nove Tocco," Tritt told me. "That was a case."

That was an understatement. In the FBI's hierarchy of catching big fish, Jack Tocco made Big Ed look like a guppy. Tocco was then the longest-serving Mafia boss in America, last of the Old School Godfathers, and head of an organized crime outfit known as the Detroit Partnership. With those credentials, Tocco had been the brightest blip on the agency's radar screen for more than a decade.

"You know, that's the major league game right there," Tritt said. "It was a big wiretap case, a long trial. That's what we get paid to do, so we just kind of put everything else on hold."

Tocco's arrest along with sixteen associates from the Detroit Partnership didn't just put the Fed's Ed Martin investigation on the back burner; it took it off the stove altogether. However, that gave Tritt and his people time to very slowly, piece by piece, assemble cases against Dad and me over the course of nearly two years.

In order to obtain an indictment against us, the FBI first had to gather evidence. And one of the first places they looked was in our garbage cans.

"What we did was, we came out on the nights you guys put your trash out," Tritt explained. "We did it at your house, we did it at your dad's house, and we found your tally sheets. We found a lot of the stuff. A couple of times we would come up dry, but we found records."

Damn! I knew something was up with our trash. How could I have been such an idiot? I mean, I would come outside on many trash days and it appeared as if everybody else's can on the block was still filled to overflowing while our lid was shut tight. Didn't we have more garbage the night before? Did they only pick up part of our trash?

Had I taken half a second to think about it back then and believe what I was seeing, I might have come to the conclusion somebody was going through our trash and taking out items. How could I not have been suspicious? But it was trash, you know? It never even occurred to me that anybody would be interested in ours.

I recall that my father routinely used to collect his garbage, especially all the numbers-related refuse, bring it to work with him and throw it into the dumpsters at the Ford plant. "I think he did," Tritt says. "But everybody gets lazy. No matter how operational secure you are, people get lazy."

Hell, after all this broke, we even had neighbors tell us they had seen strange cars parked down the block from our house. The cars were occupied by square-jawed white guys, in itself something strange in our neighborhood. Robin, who never liked my involvement in the game in the first place, claims I was aware of but pooh-poohed our neighbors' speculations about those sightings, or at the very least didn't see a need to talk about them. She was sure they meant something, but I just couldn't wrap my head around the idea that anybody would come here to watch us, to spy on me and my family day after day.

It was as if I had a veil over my head that prevented me from seeing... or thinking.

Agent Tritt told me I shouldn't beat myself up too badly. "Sometimes we would drive by and say, 'OK, what kind of bags are they using?' Then we would go down the street, find a neighbor who had the same kind of bag and bring it to your house because, who looks at their trash again, right?

"The other option was, sometimes we took all your garbage, sorted through it, took what we wanted and put the rest back. But a handful of times we didn't bring it back. We got lazy."

For my part, I wasn't thinking I was bulletproof, couldn't be messed with, or anything like that. It's just that I knew that for more than twenty years nobody had been prosecuted for running a numbers operation in Detroit. The biggest operator in our area, a dude called "Cowboy," got busted a year or so earlier and just paid a fine. A couple hundred bucks, and he didn't stop running his business a single day.

That's what I told my cousin, Lawrence, back when I was recruiting him to join my operation and knew he had to convince his wife. And that's what I told Robin.

"Carl, they have to be watching us," Robin kept saying.

"Oh, no, baby," I kept replying. "They got to be watching somebody else down the street. You know there's got to be some drug dealers and other kinds of criminals in this neighborhood. They all can't be on the up-and-up."

"Well, then, they've got to be watching us, too."

Robin always said I was like my father in that way. Our tendency was to see the good side of a situation and never spend time thinking about the uglier possibilities.

I hate it when she's right.

I don't want to hide behind the term "victimless crime," but I've got to believe numbers is the closest thing to it. No drugs, no violence: it's "the gentleman's game," right? People have to control their gambling jones, but nobody's holding a pistol to their head to put that number down. Consenting adults. You don't want to play, don't play.

What I failed to take into account was that when the numbers are associated with any more serious offense, suddenly it can become a major crime, too. Sometimes, the numbers operation is what the feds use to link you to the bigger felony. And Ed Martin's connection to – and fixation with – the University of Michigan basketball program was more than enough to make him, me, and anybody connected with us a blip on the government's radar.

"Our squad, the Organized Crime Squad, was responsible for illegal gambling matters," Tritt explained to me, "but they consisted mostly of, you know, traditional organized crime. The FBI's interest was based on illegal gambling businesses even though we don't work numbers as a rule. But anytime you hear about the mix of athletes and gambling, it suddenly piques interest."

The faxes, tally sheets and other information they fished out of our throwaways gave them enough probable cause to obtain an affidavit to tap our phones. They installed a dialed number recorder to collect every number we called, looking to identify those people we called frequently. Then they received discs from the phone company that contained lists of toll calls.

Click. As if someone had switched on a light, I could see clearly now. When Tritt took me through how the Feds had trapped me, it explained a lot of things. Just like the tumblers in a safe, the pieces were falling into place now, including those clicks on my phones I just wrote off to bad connections. Was I really that stupid, or just oblivious? Either way, it all came out to the same thing.

"We subpoenaed telephone toll records and loaded all that information into databases," Tritt says. "Because you know, if this had been a traditional organized crime family, we already would have had information. We would have had some sort of knowledge of who was who. On this thing, we didn't know anybody. We knew a couple of names, but we really didn't have anybody to talk to."

Or so he claimed. Suddenly, I recalled the bizarre, out-of-the-blue behavior of my main man Byron, whose house served as the focal point for the majority of my business. I was paying him $1,200 a week for his efforts, and put his girlfriend on the payroll, too: less chance of her becoming pissed off about the constant activity in her home if she was benefitting from it, too, I reasoned.

One Tuesday the previous summer, after the midday numbers were out, Byron called and said they wanted to quit. Just like that! By the time I get to his house, he was moving my equipment out through his front door, as if it had instantly become contaminated! He told me he had found Jesus and didn't want to be associated with the game any longer. Even though he put me in an immediate bind scrambling to cover his duties, I could respect his decision. That's fine.

Some time later, however, Byron called and said he wanted to talk to me. Maybe he had changed his mind, I figured, or missed that money. Even though he drove a sharp sports car, he came to pick me up in an older, nondescript sedan he also owned. Good cover, I thought to myself. But as we rode around talking, I noticed a little tape recorder on the bench style seat where the armrest comes down, like the kind we used to record incoming bets over the phone.

"Is that on?" I asked.

"Oh, no," Byron replied.

"Then why is it in your car?"

"I just came across it," he said.

I didn't press the issue, but I became very quiet and measured my words carefully. Was Byron trying to record our conversation? And if so, to what end? Did the feds get to him? Did they pressure him to try and get some incriminating evidence from me on tape? I'll never know for sure.

Meanwhile, Scartozzi, who worked for the IRS CID – its Criminal Investigative Division – had been assigned to the organized crime task force and was doing his part. "I'm really not involved in the wiretap part," he says. "My job is basically to start gathering information on Ed Martin, on Carl Martin. The FBI agents are getting their evidence off the wiretaps. I'm supporting their investigation.

"If the FBI had been investigating Ed Martin, even if all that U-M stuff hadn't been known, the IRS still would have become involved in the investigation. But did the U-M connection make it sexier? Of course."

It took the Feds months to sift through all of the detritus gathered from Dad's house, and from my places and other locations that were identified through the wiretaps. Eventually they had amassed sufficient evidence to obtain search warrants for their co-ordinated blitz raids across southeast Michigan.

For me, the worst part – the one thing that grinds my insides to this day – is that I wasn't there to protect my family. When the G-Men invaded my house like stormtroopers, Robin was at home alone with our baby girl, Kelsey.

I had left that morning to go to the bank. We had a big hit the night before and I needed to pay the winners, so I took all the checks we had accepted or cashed for other people, signed them over, and converted them to money. The tellers at my bank all knew me by name, so the transaction didn't take more than a few minutes. I walked out with about $20,000 in cash in a white bank envelope.

I couldn't have been gone from my house very long. Thirty minutes, tops.

As it happened, 30 minutes was all it took.

From left, three generations of Martins, celebrating a baptism not long before the raid: Carl, Ed holding the newest addition, Carissa, Robin and niece Keandra

Robin was home that morning. Just a week earlier, she had decided to take a leave of absence from her real estate office. I was bringing in enough money for us to live comfortably, so she wanted to concentrate on being a stay-at-home wife and mother for a while.

We made the decision before Kelsey was born to put Carissa in day care temporarily, so she wouldn't feel neglected or grow jealous of her newborn sister. It was just my wife, alone with our months-old infant girl, in our peaceful home when the Feds began banging on our front door.

Fortunately for Robin, her mother, who also had been a stay-at-home mom, had given her some good advice. "She used to say, 'Just because you are home all day, that doesn't mean you shouldn't always be presentable'," Robin recalled. "For some reason, her voice was ringing in my head that morning."

So rather than looking like she had just rolled out of bed, Robin already had showered, combed her hair, put on makeup, and dressed. She got Kelsey up and dressed, too. "Kelsey and I were looking really nice, sitting at home," she said.

In fact, Robin remembers, the day had gotten off to an ideal start. "I did the laundry, cleaned the house, everything was spotless. I was sitting on the floor in our family room playing with Kelsey, probably watching a soap opera on TV. Then there was a knock at the door."

We didn't have drapes over our living room windows. Robin picked up the baby into her arms and walked to the front room to see who was at the door. She peered out the window.

All she could see was an ocean of dark caps, bulletproof vests and giant white letters. A female officer was in the lead, standing on the porch. She was with the ATF, the federal Bureau of Alcohol, Tobacco, Firearms and Explosives, and she was the one doing the pounding. She wasn't selling magazines.

"Open the door!"

Robin did as she was told. At least a half-dozen agents, maybe more, pushed past her and into our house. "What is going on?" Robin yelled as they rushed my front room.

None of them had guns drawn, but they moved in such a way as to make sure Robin knew they were packing.

"Do you have any weapons in the house?" the ATF woman demanded. (I later found out the ATF gets involved in almost every raid in or around Detroit.)

"Yes," Robin replied calmly, "they are upstairs."

She told them where in the house our guns could be found. Several agents raced upstairs, while others made sure Robin sat on the family room couch with Kelsey on her lap.

I had several small gun safes located throughout the house. I owned a 9mm Beretta, a Glock .45 Auto, a Smith & Wesson Airweight .38, a Snub-nose .357 and a Smith & Wesson .45, among others. I wouldn't call myself a collector, but when I saw a gun I really liked I'd be more likely than not to buy it. Besides, having access to handguns in my chosen line of work was practically a necessity. I never expected to have to use one and hoped that would never happen. I wasn't licensed to carry, but all my guns were registered.

Meanwhile, downstairs, one of the agents guarding Robin asked, "Is there anybody you would like to call?"

Her first thought, of course, was, Man, was there ever! She wanted to give me a head's-up. The way Robin responded to this situation is the reason you always want a city girl as your wife if you're in the game—they can think on their feet. Robin didn't run around the house all frantic, screaming, "Oh, my God! Oh, my God! What do I do?" She was chill and levelheaded from the moment she opened the door, immediately focused on how to let people know that the heat was on.

She called my cell phone, but couldn't get through. I know I wasn't on it while I was at the bank, and even if I was I would have seen her call coming in. The Feds never admitted it, but I'm certain they had my cell phone blocked the day of the raid. Robin's and Ed's phones too, for all I know.

She told the agent her call didn't go through, so she was allowed to make another. Thinking quickly, Robin decided to call my mom from our home's landline. "At least I can warn her," she thought.

Ring. Ring. Ring. Ring. When somebody finally picked up the phone, it wasn't Hilda. It wasn't Ed, either. An unfamiliar voice answered, "Martin residence."

Damn. Too late! The Feds were already there!

"Hello," Robin said cautiously. "May I speak to Mrs. Martin, please?"

"She is unavailable to come to the phone right now. Who is this?"

"That's OK," Robin responded, hanging up fast.

After that, the agents took control of our house phone, too. Anyone who called us the rest of that day was answered by a gruff FBI agent who barked, "Hello! Who is this, please?"

We learned only later that simultaneous with the assault on our home, eleven agents had gathered outside Ed and Hilda's doorway on Fairway Drive. They were ready for trouble which even they knew was unlikely. If they indeed had investigated Dad's activities for two years, they had come to know this man had never been violent. Nevertheless, they took no chances.

Guns were at the ready. Agents took positions near doors and windows around the back and sides of Ed's home. Others staked out near shrubbery. It's go time.

"FBI! Open up!"

The shouts were repeated in rhythm with the bam-bam-bam on the door.

When there was no quick response, the voices grew harsher, more demanding.

"Open up!"

Hilda finally managed to make her way to the front door and opened it, no idea what all the commotion was about.

Agents stormed past her and into the house, hands on their holstered pistols, long guns pointed skyward. They scattered through the house like roaches when the light comes on. In just seconds they had taken control of the situation, whether it needed controlling or not.

"Who's in here with you?" someone shouted.

"My husband, and my son," Hilda replied. My brother, Bruce, was living with Mom and Dad at the time, in a secluded upstairs room past the laundry area and down a darkened hallway. Hilda didn't have time to mention he was bipolar and schizophrenic.

At that moment Ed Martin started down the staircase, and I'm sure he had to blink and look twice at the military-like onslaught in his normally peaceful living room.

Agents grabbed Ed. Others blew past him, heading upstairs.

"What's going on?" he said. "Why are y'all here? I ain't hurt nobody. I ain't done nothin' to nobody."

Mom said he kept repeating the same pleading statement – "I ain't hurt nobody, I ain't done nothin' to nobody" – over and over. A stunned, sad lament.

Meanwhile, another team of agents had made their way to Bruce's bedroom door.

Again, the rat-a-tat-tat banging on a door.

Bruce was fast asleep. He awoke with his heart in his throat.

"Who is it?"

"FBI! Come out. Now!"

"Can I get my glasses?" he asked.

"No! Come out!"

Although he had a moment to locate his eyeglasses, Bruce did as he was ordered and emerged from his room half-blind. He knew better than to defy the FBI.

Once everyone was downstairs, the Martins were placed in chairs about twenty feet apart. Hilda sat near the fireplace, Ed in his big chair next to the window overlooking the golf course, and Bruce near the dining room. This was standard operating procedure so the "suspects" couldn't share or compare their stories.

Bruce remembers that once the family was secure, agents carrying stacks of paper went through each room. They wrote a big letter on one sheet and stuck it on a wall. Then they placed the same letter on every article they removed from that room, so they could identify its location later. They put some items in plastic evidence bags with the same letters affixed.

They had to be writing their asses off when they got to Ed's office, really little more than an extra-large closet off the back bedroom. It was stuffed wall-to-wall with papers, receipts, mementos, restaurant reviews and race forms. Not knowing what might be important, agents had to tag and bag it all. You know they had to be muttering about what a pack rat my father was, but had they called ahead and let Ed know they were coming to raid him, I'm sure he would have tidied up a bit.

There was more than miscellaneous stuff in his office. The Feds found a bank bag containing $20,000. There was another $3,000 in cash, just lying about. And that was actually a light haul because on a routine day that bag might have had as much as $35,000.

At the same time all this was going down, Robin's real estate office was being raided, too. If we had known that, we might have been able to put some pieces together and more quickly puzzle out the real motive behind these raids on so many fronts.

The agents who raided our houses never specifically told us

why they were there; we just assumed it was about our numbers operations. However, Robin's brother had a girlfriend who worked in that real estate office. Later that evening, after the agents left our home, her brother telephoned us to tell Robin what his girlfriend had reported.

According to her, agents kept asking the office workers about basketball players – specifically, University of Michigan basketball players. Had they ever seen any players at the office? Did they know anything about the U-M basketball team? Did they know of any documents with players' signatures on them?

We were suspicious about the girlfriend's account because she had a reputation for stretching the truth for dramatic effect. So at first Robin didn't believe her brother's report, assuming his lady was just making stuff up. "They ain't lookin' for no Chris Webber or U of M stuff," she chided him then. Only after some time passed and other details became known did we realized she had to be telling the truth.

Finally it hit us. Our numbers game was never the primary motivation for the raid. It was only the pretext. The Feds wanted dirt on Ed Martin and his ties to University of Michigan basketball.

Meanwhile, in addition to the cash in Ed's office, agents at Fairway Drive had stumbled upon Hilda's cache of $18,000, the money she kept hidden under the carpet beneath the jewelry box in the bedroom. It was the stockpile she had built from the weekly $2,000 of "just-because cash" I was giving her.

The discovery of Mom's money sparked an explosion of anger on both sides, husband and wife. Ed was furious that he knew nothing of Mom's secret stash, and Hilda was livid that her money had been seized due to his shenanigans.

"It's *your* fault they came up in here, and now they got *my* money?" Mom raged. "You're the reason why they're here, and I've told you numerous times not to be the reason! Who's gonna pay me back my money?"

Minutes after Robin failed to connect with Hilda and Ed, I pulled into my driveway and put my car in park. Now, here's the thing that trips me out to this day: I had no idea anything was going on in my neighborhood, much less inside my own house. At that moment, everything on the street appeared completely normal and quiet.

It was only after I parked the car and started to open the door that armed federal agents seem to drop from out of the sky. They came from every direction and instantly surrounded my vehicle. Did they jump out from the bushes? Did they run around from behind the house? Where did they come from?

A car screeched up behind mine to block me in the driveway. I could have sworn there were no cars on the street when I arrived. Now there's a car in back of me, and in just seconds there were more cars on my lawn.

And then the blare of high-power megaphone:

"Driver! Stay in your vehicle! Keep your hands where we can see them!"

"Damn, y'all are pretty good.," I thought. "This is just like TV! Y'all snuck a brother pretty nice."

I don't know if they had anybody trail me to the bank or not, but they had to know I would be coming back home at some point. I wonder, did my leaving the house mess up the timing of their raid? Did they anticipate I was going to be there? Or were the G-Men actually happy that I left, because a house with just a woman and a small baby inside would be easier to invade?

That's the worst part, the one thing that still grinds at my insides: I wasn't there to protect my family. Now, I know Robin can handle herself, but those Feds blitzing my house with guns and body armor could have traumatized our Kelsey for life, even at that young age.

They put my wife and child at risk. I hate that. If they had told me they were coming, I sure as hell would have been there to meet them. No way would I want Robin to face all that bedlam by herself, while trying to protect our baby girl.

But there I was, trapped in the driver's seat of my car. By this time I was shaking. This is way more than anybody has a reason to expect in the middle of their day.

Again the blast of the megaphone: "Take the keys out of the ignition. Step out of the vehicle! Do it now!"

Probably by instinct I glanced down and to my right. The envelope full of cash. Oh, shit! The twenty grand I just got at the bank. There it was, the envelope lying on the passenger seat.

What should I do? Leave the envelope on the seat, in plain view? Grab it and put it in my pocket? At that moment, I knew I didn't really want to make any sudden moves.

So in a split-second decision, I left the $20,000 right where it was and got out of my car. That hurt. Maybe I made the wrong decision, because two agents patted me down quickly – I guess to see if I was carrying a gun or some other weapon – but no one took anything out of my pockets. They "meek patted" me. I was barely touched. I've had more intense searches from bouncers at a nightclub.

They confiscated the cash in the bank envelope, but let me keep all the money I had on me. Another bad guess on my part. I seemed to be making a lot of them.

I think they knew who they were dealing with. Obviously they had been watching me for a long time. They knew I wasn't likely to put up a fight, or whip out a piece and start blasting. I'm not a violent guy.

They didn't handcuff me. Instead, they flanked me on three sides as they walked me to my front door. As I reached to open it, still more agents came out the door from the other side.

"Damn," I thought. "Y'all are already in my house? "How does this work? What a trip."

Once inside, I took Robin and Kelsey in my arms. I held them tight. I wanted to make sure they both were all right.

After that, I didn't do much more than say "yes," "no," and get more and more pissed off. The agents just took over my house, and they seemed to go through everything in every room. At one point someone snatched up the family computer and was about to leave the house with it, but Robin protested.

"That's the computer my son does his school homework on," she explained. To our mutual amazement, the agent nodded, replaced the computer on its table and plugged it back in. "Well, OK," I thought. "At least they got a little sense."

Once they all got rolling, however, they lost their minds. They went through everything: all the papers they could find, the drawers, the shelves, crawling over every inch of every room like ants on a sugar cube. They brought me upstairs and had me open my gun safe, but let me close it without taking my guns.

At Ed's house they had seized every dollar they could find on the premises—including Hilda's—and confiscated his only handgun, but they had let me keep my pocket cash and left all my guns in the safe. It was weird how their priorities were so different in different raids.

Also strange are the things you remember at such a time, like a couple agents standing there in the kitchen, analyzing Brandon's basketball schedule on the refrigerator door.

Agents Jim Tritt and Frank Scartozzi—two men I would one day get to know better—stopped by for a few minutes but did nothing to stem the wreckage. They just wanted to see what their people were finding. They had gone by Dad's house before coming to mine, and had to look in on at least ten more locations before their day was over.

Meanwhile, their agents kept making snide little comments. I remember one of them glancing in my direction, handling my possessions and saying more than once, "I guess crime does pay."

I could feel myself seething. These bastards... putting their hands all over our things...making jokes at our expense... scaring my wife and baby... in *my* house!

Maybe they were trying to make themselves feel better with their wisecracks, since they knew I was no gangster or big-time federal crook. Maybe they were trying to bait me with their smart remarks, hoping I would blurt out something incriminating that they could use against me later. Whatever their intention, they were making me angrier and angrier with each passing moment.

It finally built up to where I couldn't take it anymore.

What turned on my switch was I had just realized that if they had come for me, I'd be in handcuffs by now. They probably had a warrant to search the Carl Martin premises, but no arrest warrant for the person Carl Martin.

"Hey, you can't stop me from leaving, right?" I shouted to no one in particular. "Can I go?"

Silence. "No, we can't hold you here," one agent finally said to me. "But are you sure you want to go?"

"I'm sure," I replied, bolting for the front door.

Now, I know I may seem like a punk, leaving Robin and Kelsey alone again with these SOBs while I ran out of the house. But like I said before, I knew Robin could handle whatever they threw at her, and I just realized I had a job to do. I was a man on a mission: I still had almost $9,000 in my pocket that the feds hadn't found with their weak little pat down, and I had to stash it somewhere fast before they changed their minds. My Aunt Lil's house was the closest place that came to mind.

I raced outside. Oh, shit! The agents' cars still had my ride blocked in my driveway! That wasn't going to deter me. I went around to the side of the house, grabbed Brandon's old bicycle and began peddling down the sidewalk. Aunt Lil's crib or bust!

It was just a little over a half-mile to Aunt Lil's place in the first block off of Seven Mile Road. Not far to go, but as soon as I started peddling, it was like going through molasses. Damn! The rear tire was flat. On top of that, maybe I wasn't in as good a shape as I thought I was. Here I am, pedaling away, huffing and puffing, sweating like a deacon in a whorehouse, probably looking like a straight-up fool. But at least I was moving, with a chance to put that $9,000 someplace safe.

I looked behind me several times while en route. No one following me. It had to be only a few minutes, but it seemed like forever before I arrived, winded and in pain, at Aunt Lil's house. As I rushed into the house, I could see that my Aunt Shirley was also there with her.

I was already heading for the stairway when I said, "Hey, I got to do something upstairs. I don't want to tell you what, because it'll be better if you don't know. But I'm gonna run upstairs for a minute, OK?"

"That's all right, baby," Aunt Lil replied, as cool as I was flushed. "You do what you got to do. I know there's a lot of stuff goin' on with y'all right now."

Here I had decided not to tell them what was going down, reasoning that the less they knew, the better. But it seemed they already knew about the raids. I shouldn't have been surprised—bad news travels fast in the 'hood.

I ran up to the third floor attic, found what I hoped would be a superb hiding place, and stuck all the money I had in my pocket inside it. I didn't much care what happened to me now. At least we had a little nest egg to tide Robin and me over in case we needed it. Now I've got to get right back to my own crib. So I said a hasty goodbye to my aunts and jumped back on that raggedy-ass bicycle. I didn't sweat quite as much on the return trip, probably because the anxiety over stashing the money had passed. But that damned tire was no less flat on the return trip.

Meanwhile, while I was out of my house, some of the agents had tried to work on Robin.

"Do you have anything you want to tell us?" one asked her.

"Anything like what?" she answered.

"You know, anything you think we should know, to help you out?"

"No," she said simply.

According to Robin, that was about the extent of the conversation while I was gone. She didn't speak to them, and except for the string of mocking comments they tossed in our direction, the agents didn't say much to us the entire time they were there. They were extremely businesslike. Careless, invasive, destructive, rude... but businesslike.

In the midst of this three-ring circus, Brandon arrived home from school. He was riding his newer bicycle, the one with two inflated tires. As he approached the house, he must have seen the cars parked on our lawn, noticed Feds with big logos on their jackets, and, through our picture window, seen the cluster of Caucasians milling around in our front room.

Brandon had no way of knowing exactly what was going on, but he knew it wasn't the Publishers Clearing House prize patrol coming to give us a giant check.

His first instinct, and it was a smart one, was to keep pedaling past our house. He could hang out with one of his buddies down the street until he could call us or figure out what was happening. That plan actually might have worked, until he heard...

"Brandon! Stop! Where are you going?"

"Oh, my God," he thought. "They know my name! What the hell is going on here?"

Terrified, Brandon stopped instantly, then turned his bicycle around and cautiously headed back to the house and came inside.

At some point during the chaos, we had another visitor. It was Wright Blake, a prominent Detroit attorney and an associate of mine. He had heard about the commotion (and by then, who hadn't?) and came to see if he could be of assistance. He wasn't my attorney, but I would soon come to wish he was.

Blake made it all the way to our front porch, possibly by flashing his credentials, and since I was free to come and go, I stepped outside to greet him.

He shook my hand, looked me in the eye and said, "Are you guys alright?'

I said something or other, then asked, "What do you make of all of this?"

"Well, somebody is going to do some time behind this."

I thought to myself, "Who? Who's going to do time? Is he talking about me?"

Blake had seen a lot more of this kind of situation than I had and he surmised that the Feds had invested too much time, planning, manpower and money to go back empty-handed to their superiors. Even seeing just this one site of a sweep of a dozen places raided, he knew we were caught up in a major operation. Eventually, somebody – maybe a whole lot of somebodies – was going to be the scapegoat.

Eddie L. Martin, it appeared, had long since been selected as Scapegoat No. 1.

Finally, the stormtroopers departed from my home, unblocking my car as they did. Mobile now, I jumped in the car and drove over to my parents' house to check on Mom and Dad. As harrowing and humiliating as our experience had been, I managed a little smile. The Feds had completely trashed my place, but somehow they missed something. They had failed to find the $8,000 I had stashed in the box of a special collector's doll on a shelf in our daughter's bedroom closet.

I was going to need that too, and probably a whole lot more.

When I entered my folks' house, I instantly saw how shaken my Mom, Dad and Bruce were. I was angry and heartbroken in equal measure to see my family so rattled.

As in my case, the Feds had no warrant for Ed's person. But they had placed my father, mother, and brother in handcuffs and trampled over every square inch of their home. My parents had to watch as agents hauled out thousands of dollars of their money with impunity, and towed away Ed's 1994 silver Mercedes S500. The G-Men had left my people trembling.

I got back into my car and drove home. I re-opened a small gun case and retrieved the Snub-nose .357; it was similar to my father's weapon the agents had confiscated. Then I drove back to Fairway Drive.

Dad was sitting looking dazed when I went up and handed the Snub-nose to him. I knew it was unlikely someone would break into a house that the FBI, IRS and ATF have just departed. But I figured for one night, Ed Martin – who almost never asked for emotional support – needed something to hold on to.

CHAPTER FOURTEEN

Choosing Sides

One of the first things kids learn in after-school pick-up games is choosing sides and what it means to be on a team. When you're accepted onto a team, an implicit bond is formed. The team has your back; they deserve and depend on your loyalty in return. This bond is unwritten. It might never be stated aloud. But that bond becomes the code you live by. The sanctity of code instilled in grade school can influence major life decisions many decades later.

In the days following the raids, every local station and news media outlet you can think of had congregated outside the front door of the Ed Martin house. You would have thought the Pope was in town and stopped by to pay Dad a visit.

The three majors – ABC, NBC and CBS – were represented on the lawn, as was every national cable news operation. The only network I can think of that wasn't in attendance was the one you might most expect to be there today: "the worldwide leader in sports," ESPN. Let me assure you, however, ESPN definitely was heating up my Dad's house phone. We never figured out how ESPN got that phone number.

But it soon became obvious that there was a gaggle of others who were certain they had Big Ed Martin's number – nearly every sports radio jock, newspaper and magazine writer, and whatever would-be pundit who crawled out of the woodwork.

As if I wasn't already aware that the situation was totally surreal, then HBO called. H-Freakin'-B-O! I will never forget that moment. On the other end of the line was Armen Keteyian, fellow Detroiter and, at the time, featured correspondent for the HBO Sports show, "Real Sports With Bryant Gumbel." He was offering an HBO special in exchange for exclusive access to Ed for a one-on-one interview.

Now, HBO Sports specials are fairly commonplace but in the late 1990s they were rare. Clearly, Keteyian was positioning himself to be the point man for telling and interpreting Ed's story to the world. My reaction to the offer?

"Whoa." Already this was building into an over-the-top media circus. Now here comes Keteyian, anointing himself the ringmaster. What did that make my father? The dancing bear?

Everyone wanted the exclusive. Suddenly everybody wanted to hear Ed's side of the story. Yet could anyone from the national media ever really imagine that this savvy, street-smart numbers czar would even talk to the Feds, much less to them?

That is, until the love of his life was threatened.

Big Ed wouldn't talk for money. He wouldn't talk to clear his good name. And he certainly wouldn't talk to wiggle himself out of his legal entanglements. But when it came to Hilda, he was ready to sit down and answer any question the government asked.

It has become a time-honored ploy for prosecutors. It's probably on the first page of the Prosecutor's Playbook: threaten to come after someone close to a suspect. It's especially effective if that happens to be a spouse or lover. They'll even threaten going after son or daughter if that will extract the information they want.

No disputing this technique is effective. The suspect knows that if he or she is incarcerated, the loved one will be the anchor for the family. So, when the Feds pressured Ed Martin by threatening to include Hilda, his cancer-stricken wife, in their prosecution,

Dad caved. What choice did he have? He told them anything and everything they wanted to know, but I'm certain the experience left him feeling humiliated and emasculated.

Exactly what did Ed Martin tell the Feds? Those basketball players who had been the beneficiaries of his generosity, as well as the people involved in his numbers game, undoubtedly spent sleepless nights tossing and turning over that very question. But the answer can never be known, only speculated about, because the one man who really knows is gone and the Feds either don't have the detailed records of those interviews or will never make them available. He obviously told them enough that they agreed to drop all charges against his Hilda.

In the midst of all this confusion, the news media trucks sat parked outside my parents' house, putting out a constant rumble from their ever-idling engines and pumping pollution into the air. Press reporters milled around, hoping their competitors had no more inside scoop than they did. Meanwhile, inside the house, the Martin family members tried to console each other even as they struggled to accept just how bad the situation was.

Someone knocked on the door and I immediately got up and got pissed off. We had made it very clear to all the media outlets to stay the hell off our property. I can still remember hearing that knock and seeing the entire family flinch at the sound. Then someone had the nerve to ring the bell, too! Now, furious about it, I made a beeline to the door, primed to take out all my anger on whatever damned fool was disrespecting our privacy. It might not do any good, but it would sure make me feel better.

When I opened the door, instead of some rude stranger, I saw a very familiar face. Such a kindly face – someone I knew and liked and for what seemed like forever I somehow couldn't put a name to that face. Mercifully, an instant later my over-loaded brain made the connection and I welcomed Frank Lenard, father of Voshon, one of the Southwestern stars my father had supported and counseled.

Frank beamed, shook my hand and immediately apologized for being so late.

"Late for what?" I thought to myself. "What's he talking about? We were raided almost a week ago."

Frank went on to tell me he'd been thinking about us. Then he asked if he could see my Dad. I asked him to please wait a minute and walked over to the family room, where my father sat, his head buried in his hands.

When I told him who was at the door, he looked up, almost dazed, as if he couldn't quite process what I had said. I smiled at seeing an old familiar look of pleasant surprise in his eyes once again. It had been less than a week since the April 28 raid but it seemed as if we had been dealing with this new reality forever. It had been a soul-shattering five days for the Martins. And looking at my father, it had already taken a physical toll as well.

Dad rose from his chair and, wondering what Frank had come to tell us, we walked to the front of the house where he was waiting. There is that moment sometimes in life when you can't possibly know what is about to happen, yet somehow you just know it's going to be good. I hadn't had many of those moments lately, but I sensed this was going to be one.

The first thing Frank asked was how we were holding up under all this duress. He wanted us to know that until this day he had no idea we had been raided. "I just didn't know," he said. Then he proceeded to tell us how thankful he was for all the times we stepped up for his son. Looking into my father's eyes, he told him he knew that Ed Martin was always there for Voshon, always supporting him in every way he could. Ed went so far as to have my brother Bruce personally tutor Voshon to make sure he obtained a high enough score on his ACT so he would able to play ball his freshman year. Frank would never forget all he had done.

I saw how those words moved my father. This was the kind

of sentiment he so longed to hear, but for whatever reasons, had heard so seldom over the years.

Voshon's home environment probably had been more similar to the one I grew up in than almost any other player that came through Southwestern High School in the '80s. Frank and Sandra Lenard were very active parents in Voshon's life and did all they could for their son, but as Frank talked to my father, it was obvious Voshon's parents were well aware how helpful Ed Martin's financial support and encouragement had been.

My father had known before this that the Lenards appreciated him. But now, as the Martin family was truly at its lowest point, to hear these sentiments re-enforced was priceless. Frank Lenard had cared enough to disregard the accusations and cheap shots that were being leveled in the papers and on television.

When the moment of truth came, the Lenards had stepped up and told us, "We got you, Martins. We remember all the help you gave us. We are here in your time of need."

This was a good time to let Ed and Frank talk privately, so I excused myself. A half hour or so later, I could see that their conversation, although still very intimate, was winding down.

As it came time for Frank to leave, he repeated how he and his wife felt about us, about what my father had done for their son, and for them. Then he handed my father an envelope.

"This $2,000 is currently all I have."

Dad and I just looked at each other. This man had just brought us all the money he could get his hands on.

That gesture said so much. You hear that a man who has helped you in times of need is in trouble, and you act. You don't forget. You don't turn your back. You're not selfish. You do for Ed because Ed did for you, and you know he needs your support.

"I already spoke with Voshon," Frank added, "and we will figure out a way to get you some more help. Don't you worry about a thing. We will figure it out and make it happen."

And sure enough, they did. Within thirty days, after some financial machinations, $20,000 was deposited into Robin's account, money that was earmarked to be made available to Ed immediately. Frank's words of support had come at a time they were most needed. He then followed those words with actions that demonstrated an appreciation for what Ed Martin had done over the past fifteen years.

Both were so important, the financial assistance and that acknowledgement of deep appreciation. Both were certainly needed.

In researching this book, I talked to every former Southwestern High School player from the Perry Watson era who would talk to me. In each conversation, I always asked the same two questions.

Question No. 1 – "Do you think that Jalen Rose, unlike Chris Webber, came through for Ed after he was raided?"

The immediate reply was always the same: "Yes."

Question No. 2 – "Would you be surprised to learn that Jalen did not look out for Ed after the raid, that he didn't come through in Ed's time of need?"

Again, the response never varied: "Yes."

"Well," I would then tell them, "he didn't."

It didn't matter who we interviewed from the Southwestern Prospector family, whether or not it was a teammate of Rose's. Each and every one of them had to put their head down for a moment when that truth was revealed. Their responses were eerily similar.

Each person needed a few seconds to process what Jalen, their Southwestern Prospector brother, didn't do for their beloved "uncle" when Ed Martin was at the lowest ebb in his life. They naturally assumed exactly the opposite for so many years, because it seemed so rational, so obvious. We're talking about the code here.

Why wouldn't Jalen lend a hand? Upon hearing the truth, they needed to shut out the world and roll those words around in their heads, to make sure their ears weren't playing tricks on them.

Then, a minute or so later, they were defending their brother's actions.

Understand, the love between these Prospectors who played under Coach Watson is real and palpable. They're a band of brothers, imbued with massive amounts of the mutual respect and indomitable will that comes from being part of a successful, championship-level program. I would bet the house that the Southwestern family is closer than many blood brothers.

We interviewed Rose's teammates and several other Prospector alums. These were the same teammates Jalen Rose led to two Michigan state high school championships. The same players who helped pave the way for his future success. The very brothers who savor the reflected glory from his accomplishments. And every time the question was asked about their perception of his level of support for Uncle Ed, the head would drop when that person learned his belief was false. Incomprehensible that Jalen did nothing for his Uncle Ed.

It was uncanny that all these people responded the same way. We could feel their disappointment. It was sad.

The way each of them described Jalen Rose is the way one might describe a role model or hero, the kind of ideal young man they aspired to be. They would say, Rose was always first when running sprints… always got me the ball in my favorite spot… always worked harder than everyone else at practice.

"The best team captain I ever played with," many of them said. "A great ambassador for us, and a big reason Coach got his state championships."

During those high school years, Jalen would see his Uncle Ed Martin day after day. Yes, Chris Webber saw a lot of Ed too, but there was a big difference. Jalen was well aware of what Ed did for him, and also of what he did for all his Prospector teammates as well. From his vantage point as captain, Jalen witnessed every day for four years what Ed did for every brother he played with while he was at Southwestern. He also had heard the stories of what Ed did for the players who came before him and played under P. Watt.

This is what Jalen Rose knew, perhaps better than anyone else.

Chris Webber played his high school ball at Detroit Country Day, out in Beverly Hills. He never went to Southwestern. Never was a Prospector. Never played ball for Perry Watson. Chris Webber was a big beneficiary of Ed Martin's generosity but his experience was completely different than that of many Prospector players and most especially of that of Jalen Rose.

No one knew that history better than Ed Martin. That is why he finally decided to pick up the phone and call Jalen Rose to ask for his help.

I was sitting across the table from my father when he made that call from the kitchen nook in his house. The conversation with "Jinx" – a pet name for Jalen – started amicably enough, just small talk, until about two minutes in.

"Jinx, do you know what happened over here?"

"Jinx, I'm in a tough spot here and I could use some help," he said. "What do you think? Can you help?"

I could hear Jalen's voice on the other end of the phone but could only guess at what he was saying.

"Um-hmm...um-hmmm," Dad mumbled four or five times. A long pause. "OK... we'll talk later."

He hung up the phone and sat there, silent.

From his facial expression, it was clear he did not receive the news he was hoping for.

"Dad, what did he say?"

My father stared at me as if he wanted me to explain to him what he had just heard.

"He said, 'It's too hot right now'."

We just looked at each other, letting it sink in, trying to comprehend how it could have come to this, not wanting to believe Jalen Rose had turned his back on my father.

For several minutes, we barely spoke. We knew instinctively that moving forward would be much harder from that moment on.

While we sat there, I went over in my mind the steps that my father had already taken to raise money before reluctantly picking up the phone to ask Jalen Rose for help. He had explored other options, even including going back to the ponies. That's right: Ed had begun betting on the horses again. Only this time he would not see the same results as the days when he felt certain he could go the track and walk away a winner. Because this time, Ed had no money to lose.

That's the way it is with the ponies. As they say, "Scared money can't make none." When the possibility of losing is terrifying, even the best handicapper begins to question his decisions. At one time, Big Ed Martin was one of the best around. Times change. For the first time in years, Dad needed every penny he could muster. He was now betting with scared money.

I am also certain that on some days he had success. On those days, he would bet $10,000, and when his pony came in he would walk away with $12,000.

I also remember the day he lost. Big.

Exactly how much it was I never learned. It must have been huge, because the blow it dealt was so stunning that it shook him to his core. It was almost as staggering as the day the Feds raided his house. Another big domino had toppled. Losing on the ponies made him question his reality; it struck at his very essence. That was the day Ed faced up to the reality that he could not bet on the ponies any more. He could no longer afford to lose.

With decreasing confidence – and waning options – he made that phone call to Jalen.

I give Jalen credit for even answering that phone call when

he knew it was from someone who was under federal investigation. But Ed Martin deserved more from that kid from the 'hood, from someone who had experienced and understood and received more than most. Wasn't Ed Martin due more than, "It's too hot right now?"

Man, we're talking about the code here.

Jalen Rose had violated the code. That's what my father and I were thinking as we sat in silence at that kitchen table. It was the code you live up to, no matter what, when you have grown on the streets of Detroit. It was the code that Jalen and his teammates had lived by and had reinforced daily at Southwestern:

"We are family, and family takes care of family. Family heeds that small still voice inside that says we look out for each other."

One thing Ed knew, as sure as he knew how to calculate a numbers payout, was that Jalen Rose would want to help. This was Jinx, who Uncle Ed Martin had known well since the kid was thirteen years old.

If we want to preserve our self-respect, isn't this the code we all live by?

I learned a lot in the ten years I worked on this book to fulfill my mother's request that I tell the story of Ed Martin.

For one thing, I am more aware than ever of how important parents are in the lives of their sons and daughters as they grow through their adolescence, teen years and even into their twenties. It varies, of course, but around that time in a man's life, he becomes more accountable for his actions.

That accountability is heightened when one is in control of millions of dollars. Life in that fast lane makes most people mature quickly. Jalen Rose and Chris Webber were each 26 years old in 1999 when the raid happened, well into their lucrative NBA careers. By then they were used to making their own decisions.

Dad and I had many conversations about why Frank Lenard chose to shine a ray of light for my father at his darkest hour. We wondered how much of an influence the father and son had been on each other in their post-raid actions. Often, my father and I wondered what Jalen Rose's mother, Jeanne, had said to her son. Was she aware of the code the young men of Southwestern lived by? Did Jalen get no counsel from her at all about whether to step forward, or did he get it and choose to ignore it? We knew directly and emphatically what kind of a value system Deacon Mayce Webber imparted to his son. He had left no doubt with his brutal treatment of my father in that momentous phone call at the office of Webber's lawyer.

With the Lenards at one end of the spectrum and the Webbers on the other, my father and I had real-life examples that the character young men show is often reflective of their parents and the upbringing they had.

When players from the Prospectors family were interviewed and asked what they did when they heard that Ed was raided, the answers varied widely. Some admitted that they immediately went into hiding. Others said they had tried to reach my father but didn't know how, and ultimately did nothing. As for that response, I bet if Big Ed Martin was looking to give them a $500 handshake, they would have been able to track him down.

A simple phone call, a brief visit, would have meant so much to my father during those three years of federal investigation that began after the 1999 raid. Over the course of the previous two decades Ed Martin had helped more than a hundred young men and their respective families through some tough times. All too prophetically, as my mother, Hilda, warned on countless occasions, "All those kids you are helping, they will not be there for you when you need them."

Just as my father had many sides to him, just as all men do, so did Jalen Rose. What he did – or didn't do – when my father asked for his help, that's one thing. It does not represent the sum and substance of Jalen Rose who is much more than a successful television and radio personality. He is also a generous philanthropist and a man who has demonstrated with his good works that he truly loves Detroit. In so many ways, Jalen Rose is one of Detroit's best examples of what we want our young men to grow up and become.

That said, I can still hear my father repeating what Jalen had told him on the phone: "It's too hot right now.'"

Taking that statement at face value, no question that what Jalen said makes a lot of sense. The raid was still hot in the media and fresh in the minds of Detroiters. None of the dust had settled. Yes, maybe it *was* too hot at that precise time. The thing about heat – with time, it cools off.

In early 2000 Jalen had to testify in front of the Grand Jury. A summons like that could give anyone chills down their spine. However, believe it or not, that process is so informative that once it's over, you know exactly where you stand in terms of exposure. You'll know if you're on the FBI's Most Wanted List or not. It's hard for me to believe that after testifying, Jalen wasn't fairly confident that he had no concerns. His beloved Wolverines eventually may be in jeopardy, but not him personally.

Ed Martin, on the other hand, at that time was still struggling as he refused to cooperate with the Feds and they continued to press. He made it through another Thanksgiving, another Christmas. The calendar now read January 2001. Was it still "too hot right now"? Voshon and Frank Lenard had found a way 18 months before.

I've heard Jalen express that he believes he is honoring Uncle Ed by "paying it forward," and few people are doing it better in Detroit and beyond than Jalen Rose. I have heard him talk about the values Ed Martin instilled in him, about his feelings for my father.

And that was out of sync, and remains so to this day: Among those values was the code that friends help friends. Southwestern families help their brothers. You do that especially when they are in a tough spot, because that's when they need you most.

"Paying it forward" is a great thing, but no greater than paying it back.

From the day their own house was raided, Robert "Tractor" Traylor and his family stayed connected with the Martin family. Not only that, they made sure everyone knew just how much Ed had done for them. At a time when so many people put the black hat of the villain on my father, the Traylors stood by his side every step of the way and let it be known that this man was special.

Yes, Big Ed Martin had broken rules, but Tractor and his people questioned why those rules existed. These were simple and obvious questions and yet they were hardly ever asked. Why can't a man help those who are in need? Why is it that the NCAA can make millions off the performance of poor kids, yet not put a system in place to ensure those same kids can eat, have some pocket change or get a job to help their families with bills for life's necessities?

How impertinent of them, the NCAA huffs. When are these athletes going to learn their place?

Imagine how challenging it is for a student-athlete to focus on school and athletics when he knows his family is at home hungry, with the lights or heat shut off.

Where was the NCAA leadership on this? Where are they now on this, one of the most fundamental issues of equity in all of amateur athletics? It's an issue that sports fans, alumni, and the general public increasingly see as highly hypocritical while the stakes grow ever higher, into the billions of dollars. Colleges, universities and the many interlocked and entrenched interests pour untold millions into their coffers while the athletes, who are the engine driving that gravy train, are often left to their own devices to get by and are quickly abandoned when they are no longer useful.

The NCAA has responded to these questions in ways beyond counting. The words and lofty spin varies, but it always reduces down to the same single talking point: "This is a difficult and important issue on which the NCAA places a high priority."

Translation: "We don't intend to do a damned thing about it. And now, back to the game."

So, in the absence of genuine concern by the NCAA for the plight of many of the athletes whose performances are paying their salaries, kids often are forced out of necessity to do what they have to do, to take what they have to take, to get by.

How much of that money goes back to the benefactor who provided it? If the money came from, say, the college or university itself, from an athletic apparel company, or from a pro scout, a would-be player's agent, or a professional gambler, the answer almost always is "None." Those entities have gotten – one way or another – what they want out of their "investment."

But what if the benefactor is just a private individual, a booster, say. And what of the young man on the receiving end of that generosity? How is the equity in that situation resolved? That depends on the character of the kid. As we have seen with a Chris Webber or a Maurice Taylor, it goes one way. With a Voshon Lenard or a Tractor Traylor, it goes quite another. With Jalen Rose standing somewhere in the middle.

For example, unlike Rose, Tractor continued making restitution payments to the Martins even after the cluster of coordinated raids. He fully discharged what he considered a solemn obligation by paying his benefactor Ed Martin back every penny Ed gave him and his family. Tractor held true to the Southwestern code and put action behind the words, "I will be there in your time of need," even though he was not a Prospector.

Maurice "Mo" Taylor was yet another story.

It was a saga that seemed to begin innocently enough when I introduced my father to Maurice Taylor.

Sure, in retrospect maybe I should have realized that nothing good could come from that alliance. And yes, I can rationalize it today by saying that the inevitable was going to happen anyway. If an alarm hadn't sounded when Mo rolled his car, another warning siren would have gone off another time, another place. Knowing what we know now about the priority the FBI placed on the "purity" of college athletics, their surveillance of the Martins would have begun one day regardless.

There were other consequences closer to home for the Martin family. When Mo Taylor went off the road, that rollover accident was only the first crash. It set in motion a cascade of dominoes that toppled one after the other, taking down not only the livelihood but finally the very life of Ed Martin. And yes, it left my own fortunes and freedom in the wreckage.

Within hours after the raid, my father and I knew we were up the proverbial creek and reaching out for a much-needed paddle. We met different results when we tried to call in the loans my father had made with the specific agreement they would be repaid by the players out of future earnings.

There was the heartache and anger when Deacon Mayce Webber demanded that we never contact him or Chris again... the joyous surprise of Frank Lenard's visit and unexpected checks... the crushing disappointment of Jalen claiming, "it's too hot..." the no-doubt-about-it support from Tractor Traylor. Next option was Maurice "Mo" Taylor.

By then, Taylor had been in the NBA more than two years and neither Ed nor I had heard from him since he left the University of Michigan.

After talking with several people who have been around star high school athletes for decades, I understand that very rarely does the jock remain in contact with his benefactor once his own big bank starts rolling in. It is definitely the norm that the patron has a scant chance of being reimbursed. Even knowing that, our situation was desperate enough that we had to try.

Realizing we did not have current contact info for Mo, we decided instead to start with his Aunt Sabrina, the woman who had been his de facto mother.

After we got her on the phone, it had been so long since either of us had spoken with her that we first had to catch up on life. We were saddened but not surprised when Sabrina told us that she and Mo barely talked any more. She said that lately Mo was spending more time trying to reconnect with his biological mother, Sabrina's sister.

Sure, it's understandable to try and reconnect with your mother, but in this case it is just as understandable, as well as painful, for the virtual mother to feel shunned. After all, Sabrina had been Mo's sole parent every single day when his biological mama was nowhere to be found.

There are moments in life that offer clarity. This moment, this painful revelation, was one such epiphany.

There was a recurring theme here, a script being played out again and again. Many of these players who become wealthy far beyond their childhood dreams don't just run from the boosters they owe; they run from *anyone* they owe – even their own family.

Still, Sabrina did agree to contact Mo. She said that once she had, she would get back with us. After a week passed with no word, we had about given up. Nevertheless, Ed put in another call to Sabrina.

Sabrina said she had spoken with Mo. He requested a few weeks "to think about it." She assured Ed that she had reminded Mo about what the Martins did for them back in the day. However, she clearly sensed Mo was not as receptive to her input as he had been before joining the NBA.

Two or three more weeks passed and Dad reached out to Sabrina again. This time she said she had tried to contact Mo on numerous occasions since she last spoke to us, but he was not answering. She had left several messages. Mo had not called her back.

Then Ed asked Sabrina for Mo's number. Maybe he could get through to him somehow, on some man-to-man level that Sabrina could not, even though he clearly was turning a deaf ear to her pleas. Sabrina replied that as much as she would like to give his number to Ed, she thought it best not to do so. She told Ed she would continue to call Mo until he answered or returned her call. "Give me a few more weeks," she said.

Those few weeks came and went... and a few more followed. Finally, Sabrina called Ed.

She explained how embarrassed she was that Maurice was representing himself in this way, and she really had no idea what more she could say at this point. All she could do was promise to continue contacting Mo until hopefully she received a response.

Less than two weeks later, out of the blue, Mo called Ed.

No small talk. No apology for being out of touch. If Taylor knew that our homes had been raided, he never acknowledged it. Most absent of all was any mention of his having a balance due.

He had only one reason for his call: to tell Ed to stop contacting Sabrina.

"Not a problem," Ed replied. "You pay me the money you owe me and I will stop calling your aunt. Or give me your number so I can call you directly."

Silence.

Mo had no more words for Ed. I'm sure he did not expect his warmhearted and benevolent supporter, his longtime patron, to express himself that bluntly.

The call ended abruptly. There was no plan to move forward.

A few more weeks went by and Ed received a call from a man who said he was Mo's cousin. Ed recalled having met the man once before but did not remember that he was actually Mo's cousin.

The man explained that Maurice had asked him to call. He would like to set up a meeting to discuss how Mo could repay Ed.

Of course, Dad's ears perked up. "That's great."

The cousin asked if they could meet at a place on 8 Mile Road, the thoroughfare made famous by Eminem and the road that separated Detroit from its northern suburbs, as vividly as black from white. The man said there is this strip club named All Stars. How about we get together Saturday night? Let's meet in the alley behind the club. We can talk there.

Quite a proposal, that.

Now, All Stars, which has long since been permanently shuttered, was notorious for its violent reputation and lewd activities inside the club. There had been several shootings there not long before the cousin's call. Noteworthy that he didn't suggest they meet at the corner table of a nice restaurant, or perhaps a quiet cocktail lounge, or maybe even in a well-lit parking lot. No, he proposed that just the two of them meet in the back alley of a shady dump of a bar on its loudest and busiest night.

If Mo was sending a message, it had been received, loud and clear.

The take-away was unmistakable. This is what Mo Taylor does for the man who looked out for him to the tune of $110,000. A man who provided more than $500 cash a week for four years straight? And now you want him to meet someone – not you, not your Aunt Sabrina, but your "cousin" – in a dark alley.

Dad called me to his house to get my opinion. I was stunned by what my father told me, and equally shocked that he felt the need for a second opinion. My father really felt he had to ask someone else if he should walk into an ambush? Another sign of the toll the stress was taking on Ed Martin.

Of course he needed the money, but he had been around the block enough to sense what was coming around that corner. Before this, when my father was on his "A" game, he would never have taken such a foolhardy risk just to get paid. There was another reason he was actually considering meeting this guy. Deep down he wanted so badly to believe that Mo Taylor, this prodigy in whom he had invested so much, eventually would come through. Ed Martin so desperately wanted to believe that Mo Taylor would do the right thing that he was willing to risk his life on that chance.

Not so for me. For a few minutes I was so heated I wanted to take it out on somebody. You want to entice my Dad into a dark alley on 8 Mile Road to do *what*? Discuss a realistic repayment plan? Or shoot him down like a rat? Thankfully, being accountable to my wife and kids cooled my anger.

So Ed didn't walk into an alley where he might get bushwhacked. And I didn't go after Mo or his "cousin" for satisfaction. What we did do was face up to reality and let Mo Taylor have his win.

Even though we made several attempts, we never spoke with Maurice Taylor again.

However, while doing research and interviews for this book, I spoke with several of Taylor's contemporaries. Many of them told me that was characteristic behavior, so well known among them that they had coined the phrase: "You got 'Mo-ed.'"

They used that expression whenever one of them was lied to, cheated on or deceived – not just by Taylor, but by anyone. They said Mo was so legendary for such behavior that the phrase just caught on.

Looking back, I can say, "We got 'Mo-ed.'"

In 2002, Chris Webber made a public statement during a press conference. I wish I could have been with Dad when he first saw the video, when he watched Chris's face as he said those words. But that was impossible, because I was confined several hundred miles away doing time at a minimum-security correctional facility in Pennsylvania.

But I knew my father so well I could visualize, I could feel, how it would devastate him. I could see him wince, stagger and have to sit down, looking like Michael Spinks after taking a Mike Tyson uppercut.

Here's what my father had just heard Webber say on ESPN in September, 2002:

> "This case is about a man who befriended kids like myself, preying on our naïveté, our innocence, claiming that he loved us and that he wanted to support us, but later wanting to cash in on that love and support that we thought was free."

Those words were blows to my father's spirit as well as his body, I knew his entire history with the Webbers had to be racing through his mind. The only way he could deal with what he had just heard was to delude himself with the possibility that somehow Webber really didn't mean what he said.

Ed Martin was as capable of rationalizing as any man, and perhaps more than most. So, sure, he could tell himself Chris had made those outrageous statements to distance himself. After all, Dad was under federal investigation. To get space between yourself and that stench of guilt-by-association was understandable, right? Can't fault the kid for that.

My reaction? I knew it would hurt my father if I ever blurted it out, but the cynic in me was saying, "That's just bat-shit crazy."

Even allowing for my father's rationalization to be correct, why did Chris have to so blatantly mischaracterize reality in that public statement? Why jump on the "Ed Martin-is-a-bad-man" bandwagon? Of all the ways that the Webbers hurt my father, that public smear of my father was the unkindest cut of all.

During my interviews with the FBI's Organized Crime Task Force, more than one agent declared that after investigating Chris and his father, Mayce, they were convinced that they had never encountered an individual of lower character than Mayce Webber. This revelation shed light on why Chris may have treated my father the way he did the moment he made it to the NBA. The apple rarely falls far from the tree.

Going deep into the psychoanalytical weeds of Chris Webber's motive is pointless. These were questions to which there could never be an answer. Had his father, Deacon Mayce Webber, dominated Chris all along? Was it his parents who really had been pulling the strings for the 16-year-old budding superstar? Or was Chris acting on his own initiative when he made his house call to the Martins asking for even more financial support through his high school years at Detroit Country Day? Was it solely his decision to betray my father with that public coup de grace?

We can only speculate about answers to all those questions. But it is futile to do so because it is doubtful that Chris himself really knows. Perhaps he has long since convinced himself of an alternate reality he can live with.

After all, who can doubt that many NBA athletes live a skewed reality of their own creation? It is a false reality that has been nourished by the insane amount of coddling they receive on their way to the top. From the age of, say, 14, until the day they reach the NBA, life dishes out a unique set of challenges for these physically gifted young men. They're continually told that they are special, better than everyone around them, and that people should be happy just to be in their presence. And they're bombarded by people trying to exploit them and take advantage of their talent for personal gain. That's where the boosters and the exploiters come on the scene. They have the contacts. They know how the game is played. Most of all, they have fast cash. And when cash is given, it is rarely handed out without the expectation it will come back, many times over.

Any young man who is able to navigate all these treacherous waters has to have a solid parental foundation at home. Society loads far too much pressure onto the muscled shoulders of these pampered adolescents to expect them to remain normal.

With so much attention at a young age, the star athlete begins to believe his own hype, drinks his own Kool-Aid, surrounds himself with a posse of yes men and, when his parental guidance is minimal or nonexistent, loses any sense of balance or morality in his life. Robert "Tractor" Traylor and Voshon Lenard were exceptions to this pattern. Remember: as close as Tractor Traylor was to Ed, he still called home to ask his family before committing to pay him back out of every NBA check. With his strong family foundation, Traylor was in a small minority.

Having seen it happen so many times, I have come to realize that these young superstar athletes sincerely feel used, and not without cause. Most of us never meet someone new and immediately have to wonder, "Is this person genuine, or just trying to use me?" "Does this girl like me, or does she know who I am and see me as her Big Sugar Daddy?"

No surprise then that athletes surrounded by yes men and have minimal parental guidance have a tendency to rewrite their narratives or even create entirely new ones. They convince themselves that they made it to their elevated position in life without any help at all. After repeating their newly minted narrative a few times, they buy into it so totally they could sail through a lie detector test.

CHAPTER FIFTEEN

Taking it to the Hole

On September 12, 2000, I signed a plea agreement that sent me to prison the following July. I pleaded guilty to three charges, including money laundering and tax evasion.

From the time of the raid until the day I went to prison, I was in a deep, dense fog, unable to see any future beyond the moment. I can comprehend now that I must have done things during that time, but I have no real memory of my actions. Looking at some notes on the calendars from that time, I see that I did a few real-estate transactions, but I have no recollection of the properties, the buyers or sellers, none of the details of the kind I used to know so clearly.

What I do remember doing the days and weeks and months after the raid, is sitting there… just sitting there and staring. At nothing. I learned then what it must be like for a deer staring into the headlights. For me, those headlights were the onrushing train of prison time.

That is the way more than a year passed.

One thing that occupied my mind constantly throughout those months was to try and figure out any way I could get out of going into prison. That was the one thing I clearly remember doing. I failed.

Finally, I gave up trying to find a way *not* to go. Once I resigned myself to my fate, I focused on figuring out *how* to go. I was determined to prepare my family for the inevitable. That meant setting them up for eighteen months without me or my income around.

Was it hard to get my sentence down to eighteen months? The way it seemed to me then was, if it had been hard it never would have happened. It felt that way because my attorney didn't seem particularly committed to my case. Maybe that's the way most defendants feel if they have a court-appointed lawyer. But I had a high-priced defense attorney, Neil Fink, who came with a sizable reputation. And here I was up against the Feds who were determined to get the maximum out of a very high visibility case that had consumed a lot of time and taxpayer money. It seemed to me that if I had a real aggressive and determined lawyer we should be able to negotiate the prison time down even more. Instead, here the lawyer who literally had a chunk of my life in his hands was like, "Whatever."

And I'm saying to myself, "That's all you got?"

My wife, Robin, agreed. "He wasn't trying to fight," she said. "He really understood that we had very little leverage. We thought it was laziness, but I think really he just understood that we couldn't beat them."

As usual, Robin nailed it. I had underestimated the importance of the ongoing relationship factor. Defense attorneys have to deal with the same federal prosecutors over the years, on countless cases. Attorney Fink wasn't about to cash in any favors for me that he might need for bigger fish down the road.

About that time, Robin and I were entertaining the idea of obtaining a reverse mortgage, just to have a little cash reserve against my uncertain future. So we applied, were deemed to be great candidates, and the bank set about processing the paperwork. Finally, something was going in our favor. Right up until the bank hit the brakes.

"They found out," Robin and I said to each other.

Apparently, the lender's concern was that our house eventually could be attached to some kind of federal indictment, or that it could be seized. If so, the bank could be left holding an empty bag. So rather than get involved, they walked away, quickly.

As for other assets, I still owned a few modest houses Robin could sell while I was gone and she had a real estate business that was relatively successful. She also was fixing up a property that I had purchased just before the raid, a big old two-family house. Nothing major there, but at least a few potential revenue streams and the means to get them done.

I was able to negotiate a deal that would produce about $5,000 every month for Robin while I did my time in jail. Would the Feds find it as ironic as I did where that money would have to come from? Didn't they realize I would have to sell to another numbers game house 25 percent of the business I had built? That was money from the very activity for which I was going to do time.

Throughout those days, in addition to the well-being of my own family, I was concerned about my mother and father. Ed and Hilda had his pension from Ford. Nobody could take that away. He also had Social Security benefits. He told me, "You know, I'm going to live as long as I live." Knowing my Dad's taste for maintaining a certain lifestyle, I knew what he meant. But I wondered if he would be able to do it.

On the plus side, he didn't have a mortgage. His house was paid off. The only thing he owed was an equity line on his house, about $25,000. He had taken out that debt soon after the raid just to give himself some extra cash, some money to maneuver with.

In some ways, I was more concerned about Mom and Dad's welfare while I was going to be away than I was about my wife and children. I had faith that Robin could handle things, make the right decisions so that she and the kids would be okay.

Some of our friends knew what we were going through as we prepared for me being incarcerated. One woman came over to our house early on, trying to offer words of consolation. "You know, it ain't that bad," she said. "Anybody can do a year. Right, Robin? There are a lot of women out there who are single mothers."

"Yes," Robin answered. "I was one before Carl and I got married. A year without his income, a year without my confidant, a year without my support system, and a year without my best friend. Yeah, anybody can do that."

Robin made her point that going through something like what we were facing might look like a piece of cake to someone looking at it from the outside. But the more important point in our situation was that our well-meaning friend was actually right: If anybody could do it, Robin could. She had a child before we got married. She had been a single mother before and knew that wasn't easy in our society. It was going to be especially tough during the time we were facing, now that we had more children.

As for what people might say about me being a convicted felon about to do time, I wasn't worried about that. We're from the Detroit's east side, where there's a certain level of tolerance – almost a higher threshold of acceptance – of crime. It's like everybody understands that you gotta do what you gotta do. But Brandon, our oldest, was in high school: I was worried about how he might be treated.

All good things must end, the saying goes. Fortunately, so must all bad things. Finally, this difficult passage, this pre-prison preparation, we had been going through since the raid on April 28, 1999 was about to end. We were now into the home stretch before I'd start doing my stretch.

I was sentenced to the Schuylkill Federal Corrections Institution & Camp, a minimum-security correctional facility in the tiny Pennsylvania town of Minersville, in Schuylkill County. Until the day of my sentencing, I had never so much as heard of the place.

I didn't even know how to spell Schuylkill, but I soon found out: p-r-i-s-o-n.

Whose bright idea was it to have me sent that far away?

"No, y'all got to send me somewhere closer than that. How can my family come to see me?"

But then, someone said to me, "You probably don't want to be anywhere closer."

"Why? Why can't I go to Indiana or someplace like that?"

"Overcrowded. Besides, Schuylkill is actually all right. Their camp is very nice."

Now that was something to look forward to. If ever there was an oxymoron, it had to be "a very nice prison camp."

The federal guidelines state that prisoners are supposed to be housed within a certain distance from their home. Pennsylvania was clearly far beyond the boundary for Michigan, but if they wanted to, the Feds could come up with a boatload of reasons to make an exception to that rule.

They told me I could go through all the paperwork and hassle of requesting a change of facility. But I was in the throes of my crisis of confidence in Neil Fink, my attorney, and I saw scant chance of that going through.

What should I do? I asked people I knew for their opinions, their suggestions. Someone reinforced what I had heard before, "Yes, it's a little farther away, but from what I've heard, you'll probably be better off there."

In my mind, that pretty much slammed shut the iron gate for me. From that point on, it's like you're already in prison. Physically in Detroit, but mentally I'm counting down the days and might just as well already be in prison cell.

Because I was self-surrendering, the prison gave me a day and time to report. They don't care how you get there; they expect you to be there on time. Be advised, you don't want to be late.

We didn't tell the kids where I was going. Brandon knew, of

course. He had bicycled himself right into the raid. But we felt the other two were just too young to understand. We told them I was going off to a school in Pennsylvania for a while to learn to build houses, but that I would be coming home as soon as I graduated. As far as I know, Brandon never told them the truth.

Carissa was in second grade at the time. One day her teacher was reading the newspaper in class and saw a story about a man name Ed Martin, accompanied by his photo. Carissa was standing by her desk, took a look and announced, "Hey, that's my grandfather!"

The teacher didn't believe her, and told her so. Later the teacher called us and we confirmed that our daughter was telling the truth. Eventually Carissa cut that picture out of the paper and did a current-events report to the class on her granddad, but she never made the connection between Ed's situation and the fact that I was leaving.

But leave I did.

Finally, ten months after I had signed my plea deal, it was time to go. On a hot July day, Robin, Brandon and I boarded a plane and flew to the facility that would be my "home" for the next phase of my life.

What an unforgettable flight it was from Detroit to Hershey, the closest airport to the prison. From there we would rent a car for the one-hour drive to our destination. Man, I have never had a more unsettling, weirder flight than that one. I couldn't stop thinking, "I am flying myself to prison. I bought the ticket with my own money to pay my own way into prison."

We got to Hershey the night before my appointed turn-yourself-over date. We drove the rental car to the hotel were we would spend my last night of freedom for how long a time I couldn't be certain. After we checked in, one thing I knew: I sure could use a drink. Forget that one. I couldn't have a drink the night before, because I wasn't supposed to have anything in my system the next morning when I checked in.

I've spent more enjoyable evenings than my last one as a free man in that Hershey hotel, sitting and staring into space, then tossing in bed, all the time worrying and waiting for dawn to come.

The next morning we drove Minersville in Schuylkill County, where we found our way to Schuylkill FCI & Camp. So this will be my local geography the other side of the prison walls, I thought. This is my new hometown as I do my time in a minimum-security correctional facility near a little Pennsylvania town I had never heard of until after my world came crashing down around me.

As ordered, we got there on time. As we drove up and looked at the place, all I could say was "Damn! Did I get lied to in Detroit?" My future place of residence was bleak, foreboding, heavily fortified. It was, well, prison. That part I got. Now, where was the "very nice." I don't know why that shocked me so. That's what prisons are.

I walked to the gate, approached a guard and said, "I'm Carlton Martin, here to self-surrender."

"Not here, you're not," the guard said.

"Huh? What do you mean?

"You're up the hill. This is medium security. See these fences, the barbed wire? I don't think this is where you're supposed to be but I'll check."

While he went to a desk and riffled through some papers, I looked up at the 15-foot high walls, razor-sharp wire and the guard tower. There would be guards up there with guns, I'm imagining. I'm thinking, *The Shawshank Redemption*. Robin was still in the car, waiting. I wondered what was going through her mind.

The guard made a phone call, then returned.

"Yep, I was right. You're supposed to be up the hill. That's where the prison camp is."

Whew! I felt like I'd been paroled already!

We drove around the medium-security facility and up the hill.

As we approached I saw men dressed in kitchen whites, sitting on picnic tables, smoking cigarettes. There were no gates or fences. The exterior walls of the prisons on either side formed the boundaries of the area. I started to get cocky. "Yeah," I thought to myself, "this is where I'm supposed to be."

I looked at Robin and saw that her expression brightened dramatically. It went from despair to not happiness, but to an acceptance that hey, you're going to be here a while, and this may not be too bad after all. It was a whole different feeling.

Robin remembers that moment as clearly as I do.

"We drove right past it when we were coming in," Robin recalled. "We got off the freeway and drove down these beautiful hills. You see wild turkeys and gorgeous trees. We saw these guys at a picnic table sitting around, but we kept driving because we saw barbed wire and men with guns drawn ahead of us, and we figured that's where we had to go."

We had now gotten to that dreaded moment when we had to say goodbye. It was as hard a thing to do as I had ever done. And then, Robin was gone. Back in the car, driving back to the airport. Back to Detroit and a life of coping without her partner. Back to a life I wouldn't re-enter for many months or perhaps even years.

Alone, I entered the processing-in building. I went in with just the clothes on my back. No personal possessions permitted. Your driver's license, personal ID, anything else you surrender it during processing. They took my clothes. I put on the standard-issue prison garb: khaki shirt, khaki pants, and a pair of work boots. When I walked out of that building, I became something I had never been before, something I never foresaw that I would one day be: a prisoner.

They had given me one option only and I turned it down. If you didn't want to wear boots all day, they would issue you a pair of flat, woven Asian-style sandals. One more thing I was surprised and pleased to hear was that in two weeks I could buy shoes and other merchandise at the commissary.

"I got to wear this shit on my feet for two weeks? Y'all don't know me."

But wear those boots I did. I used them to walk me right in to get myself some lunch.

It was in the eating room that I heard the first words a brother would say to me in prison.

"You got to wrench that."

"Excuse me. What?"

"You need to wrench that."

"Oh, rinse. What, you mean my cup?"

"Yeah, rinse out all your shit."

At that moment, it hit me. Damn, I'm really in prison! I'm being given instructions on how to eat.

I thanked him and rinsed out my cup, filled my little glass with ice and water and sat down. As I soon learned, prisoners who had been assigned the kitchen detail are supposed to wash all the dishes and silverware. That's their job, but some of them really don't give a damn about how well they do it. So it was wise to give a final rinse to everything you were going to eat or drink from.

That was one of my first wake-up calls. Just weeks ago, I was dining in some of the finest restaurants in Detroit. Now I've got to rinse off my fork before I can eat.

The brother, who I later came to know as Kurt, then gave me another piece of advice. "Man, you just sit anywhere you want to around here," he said. "This ain't nothin'."

I thanked him again for helpful advice. I was learning that just walking in the door cold you don't know much of anything. Like, are there cliques or a pecking order or some kind of unwritten Schuylkill cafeteria rules? You don't want to ruffle any feathers your first day in the place. But maybe this was different than what you would expect in a higher-security prison facility. This was prison, no disputing that, but it had a difference. It was prison camp.

Before I walked into this place for my confinement, I didn't really know what to expect, but it wasn't this. I realized that for one thing I wasn't the least bit scared. Actually, the emotion I was feeling was totally unexpected because I was fascinated. The people I had encountered thus far had all treated me decently and, ironically, the place seemed so open there was this sensation of almost freedom.

If you were convicted of murder, you couldn't serve your time there. But for any offense below that, if you had a great lawyer or had served "good time" elsewhere without causing any trouble, you were eligible to go to camp. The camp inmates were people who knew how to act right. We had one guy who had been imprisoned for 18 years, was convicted of kidnapping, and shot at the police while being arrested, and yet he qualified for camp because he had served "good time."

No, I didn't take pictures of the place to remember it by, but I can still describe it: Schuylkill Prison Camp is a beautiful, almost pastoral place, set in the rolling Pennsylvania hills. I wouldn't go as far as to call our camp a Club Fed, but it was wide open. There was one long, straight hallway that ran through the entire facility. We had a TV room. In fact, people there knew who I was because updates on Ed's story still ran occasionally on newscasts or ESPN.

The complex was built in 1991 to house about sixteen hundred inmates at minimum security. It was operated by fewer than three hundred staff, including guards, administrators and all other employees. The minimum-security camp housed three hundred or so inmates. As prisons go, it was a pretty safe place. There were no incidents of deaths to staff and less than a couple dozen inmate-on-inmate assaults per year. Schuylkill was one of almost one thousand minimum-security prisons in America. It's no news flash that the United States has by far a higher percentage of its citizens confined to prison than any other supposedly advanced country in the world, a high proportion of them for non-violent crimes.

Just on the other side of those 15-foot walls from me, in the medium-security building, three prominent crime bosses were doing life for multiple murders, kidnapping, extortion, drug dealing, and a laundry list of crimes. From where we lived in minimum security, they might as well have been on another planet.

I had no idea how Schuylkill compared with those other minimum-security prisons, but it seemed in the early going that I could have easily done a whole lot worse.

I mean, we even had bocce courts! In no time at all, I was hanging out on those courts with the old-boy network. Most of the bocce players were little Italian dudes that you just knew had mob connections. Here they were, friendly as could be, out on the courts for a few rounds of bocce. Sure enough, they wouldn't have it any other way, so I learned how to play.

Then there was something that reminded me of old times watching Dad dusting-up family and friends on his pool table with the window that looked out on the fairways of Detroit Golf Club. One of the old inmates was a pool shark. Nobody could ever beat him. But I was glad my father wasn't in there with me to find out.

We had plenty of stuff, actually, and things to do to kill time. We had a little basketball court, even softball leagues. We had a home field advantage, you might say, because we weren't available for road games.

I'd like to tell you that a brother from Detroit who grew up steeped in basketball dominated the court, but I'd be telling you a lie. A couple of guys from down the hill were pretty good. One brother, who went by the nickname Ham, was 6-foot-9. Just throw it in to Big Ham, baby. Sweet game, that Big Ham.

On the court, I just did what I can do. "Kick it out to me in the corner, dudes." If I'm on, we're all going to be happy. When I'm hot, I'm hot. If I'm not, quit throwing it to me. We won a lot, though, so it was all right.

I had Robin send me $300 every month. A percentage of that

went to phone minutes so I could call her, and you had to buy your own gym shoes, sweats, stuff like that. You never knew what you might need.

My first day there, I had been assigned to a bunk. There were two bunk beds to a space, upper and lower. The privileged ones, or the people with seniority, got to sleep on the bottom bunk. Far as I was concerned, I much preferred sleeping on the top. That way, wasn't nothing above me but air and ceiling. I didn't have anybody farting on me, or dropping stuff on my head, or anything like that. Top was tops in my book.

It soon occurred to me you couldn't accurately refer to us as inmates because – as I was surprised and happy to discover – I had the freedom to go outside anytime I wanted, 24/7. So we had bunkmates and mine was this young and huge Mafia dude. He was part of the crew that already was in there, but he was the most recent arrival.

He was one big dude. I could have nicknamed him "Chainsaw" but not for the reason you might think. So I just thought of him as Big Snoreboy. I remember being a little intimidated when I first walked in, but then Big Snoreboy presented me with a fruit cup. Aw, a cell-warming gift.

He also offered me popcorn and a few other food items. He said, "You won't be able to go to the commissary for a while, so in case you get hungry here's something to munch on."

I thought, "I got a fruit cup! That's cool as hell. My welcome-to-prison present!"

Maybe it was because Big Snoreboy was so massive, he must have had over-sized nasal passages and lungs. Whatever the reason, every night his snores produced the sound of a giant chainsaw ripping through our room. That was tough, man. I slept a little bit, but then again, I never slept very much at night anyway. Maybe five or six hours back home and now I was not getting even half of that with my roaring roomie below me. Even though I don't smoke, I would go outside for a "smoke break" just to get a break from all that noise.

Even being able to do that, just walk out in the middle of the night to get away from a snoring roommate, that was something I never would have expected being able to do. That's why I have to smile when people ask me, "After all you'd been through, how did you feel when you heard that cell door slam shut for the first time?"

Their eyes go wide when I tell them I never had the experience. Never once did I hear that unmistakable, hope-crushing slamming sound. Yeah, there were doors, but not the heavy metal kind you've seen in prison movies or if you've had the misfortune of hearing that sound close up and personal yourself.

Prisoners lived in huge rooms with living areas separated by walls that were about five-feet high. You could peep over them, piss over them, throw shit over them, whatever you wanted, and dudes did. It wasn't uncommon for someone to yell, "Man, give me one of them," and see something thrown to a man three or four bunks down. This was way, way below even medium security.

Not only could I go outside to escape Big Snoreboy, but initially I could also catch up on my sleep during the day. You don't have a specified job or any responsibilities when you first arrive at Schuylkill, so you're just there. Nothing to do. Might as well sleep.

A guard might say to you, "Hey, come out here and pick up these cigarette butts." Hey, activity! So I would take a little bag and go police the yard. That's the kind of menial stuff you do when you first get there. So whenever you saw someone picking up cigarette butts, you knew they were brand new. You get to know everybody in about a minute anyway.

Everybody had a job, and there were jobs to be had all over the prison. Some people cooked, some cleaned. My first job after policing up the yard was working in the prison power plant. One of the best things about that gig was I had to walk half a mile to get there. That was an incredibly liberating feeling. I had to leave early in the morning to be there on time and I walked there alone, clearing my head, feeling a little bit like a free man. Then, the colder it got, the longer that walk felt every day. I started thinking an inside job closer to camp might be nicer.

I'm naturally inquisitive, so I asked around: What's a good job? Clerk, was the reply.

"What's that? What does a clerk do?" I asked.

I soon found out.

Eventually, I was able to get transferred to the tool room, and tool room clerk was a great job. Once again along this crazy trip, I had benefitted from some good advice.

I would go every day and just sit in the room. Schuylkill had a wide assortment of tools available to the inmates because they performed various tasks around the complex. When someone came in to borrow a tool, we would "chit them out." I would take the piece of equipment off the wall, replace it with the man's chit, his prison number, fill out a card and release the tool to him. At the end of the day, or whenever the con completed his job, he brought the tool back and we reversed the process. Piece of chocolate cake.

Every piece of equipment had to be accounted for. Even though we were serving something less than even minimum security, you didn't want a prisoner running around the yard with a sharp tool. Twice it happened that I couldn't leave the tool room and go back to my bunk when my shift was over because a tool had not been returned.

So we waited. It was less than an hour both times before the lost tool was recovered. It had fallen off a table, or been placed somewhere and forgotten about. But because we were the toolroom clerks, the tools essentially were our responsibility.

One time, a blade went missing: one of those utility knives with a retractable blade. That was not good. I could see why there might have been some concern over that. But why would you let a prisoner – any prisoner – run around unsupervised with a blade in the first place?

That shows how loose things were there. Working in the kitchen, a dude could smuggle out a knife if he wanted to, no problem. It was even possible to sneak off the prison grounds if you were willing to take the risks. A lot of the guys were local, and I remember some of them would sneak out of camp after the late count at midnight, go get their groove on with their woman at a nearby motel and get back before the morning count at 4 a.m. That didn't give them a lot of time, get on down and get on back.

I didn't even think about doing something that stupid. I can understand it if you're in for, say, 20 years and you don't much care about the consequences, but I was doing short time. I only had 18 months – I hoped – to serve and a beautiful wife and family to go home to. No damn way was I about to do anything that might jeopardize my situation and get me transferred or lengthen my sentence. Why even take that chance?

After all the movies I had seen, books I had read, and stories I had heard about life behind bars, I must have subconsciously expected to be exposed to some heavy-duty violence. I remember all those images from before I entered the system to do my time. The reality I came to experience was turning out to be much different.

What was the worst thing I saw? There were a couple of fights but I'd seen a whole lot worse back on the streets in Detroit. As for just crazy-ass doings, not much of that either. There was one dude who took some laundry bags and patched them together to make dresses out of them, then paraded around like a woman.

But something that did live up to the advance expectations were the characters. There sure were plenty of them, and all kinds. You had what I called "poor dope dealers," because if you sold dope, got busted and ended up in a joint as cushy as Schuylkill, you didn't sell enough quantity to be anything but poor. You did it, but obviously you weren't very good at it. However, if my own experience had taught me, if you had a modern-day Perry Mason as your lawyer or had served your sentence down to below five years with good time and weren't a murderer, you were a candidate for the camp.

About three months in, I got a new bunkmate. Ali was a young, green-eyed brother I had gotten to know. He had mad respect out on the street and his reputation earned him the same respect from the inmates.

"Man, I had a cell by myself, but I hear one of the older guys is about to be transferred over here," Ali explained. "I don't know him, and I don't want him in with me. But I know you. The head guard will let you move in with me if you ask him. You ask him can you move, I'll tell him I want you to move, and see what they do."

I did. He did. And in no time at all I moved in with Ali.

It was cool. I didn't have a problem with him. Ali knew all the guards well, didn't cause any trouble, and we got along fine as bunkmates. He was there when I got there and he was still there when I left, so he had become kind of resigned to life in the camp.

"Only thing is, you got to take the top bunk," he insisted.

"Cool," I replied. "That's what I want anyway. Ain't no better place to be."

Maybe he wanted the bottom bunk so he didn't have to jump down to get to his prayer mat five times a day.

Ali was a practicing Muslim, and while we rarely talked about religion and he made no overt attempts to convert me (or anyone else at the camp, as far as I could tell), he inspired by his example. His daily dedication to prayer and reading the Qur'an were extraordinary.

I wasn't the only one who noticed. Because of the good time qualification, there were some inmates in Schuylkill who actually had been convicted of some serious crimes. That included a lot of white-collar criminals. There was a white guy – I seem to recall his name was Bill – who had been vice president of at least two Fortune 500 companies. It was said he was a millionaire many times over, and that was easy to believe whenever his wife came to visit him, drenched as she was in jewels and furs like a Hollywood legend.

Bill obviously had a sweet life waiting for him whenever he got out. That's why I was shocked to overhear his conversation with Ali one afternoon.

He told Ali that he truly admired him because of his spirituality. "That's something that is missing from my life," Bill said. "I've never had that sense of faith, and it's in situations like these when you really understand how important it can be.

"Yes, I've got some money, but it doesn't do me much good now. But I can see that your spirituality, your religious beliefs, are carrying you through this ordeal."

Wow. I doubt that Ali converted Bill to Islam, but just the fact that he wanted what Ali had and knew that all his riches couldn't buy it. That was insight to take away with me after I had done my time.

Ali had this tough outward image. Granted, he probably thought he needed it to survive in his environment and do his own thing. But he had something more important than that – he had a big heart. One thing he would do, he would cook a little something almost every weekend. You could get ingredients from the kitchen if you were ambitious and could put a dish together. Ali would do that, and heat it up in the community microwave we all shared in the TV room. He would boil dumplings and stuff them with whatever he could find, or make some vegetable dish. For some reason, he loved how I fixed up the tuna we could buy from the commissary and asked me to whip up a batch of my special "Detroit tuna fish" whenever I could.

There was another use for tuna in the camp – and it wasn't just as food. Tuna fish cans and gambling. Who would have thought?

Was gambling going on inside Schuylkill? What do you think? A bunch of men with time on their hands and a hunger for some action?

There was a guy there named Billy, a white dude from the Baltimore area, who had been busted for drugs. This was not Bill, the CEO with the jewel-encrusted wife, but Billy the brother from Balto. I'd become close to Billy at camp and he told me he and his boys also ran the sports book and were in charge of gambling in that area. He was still hustling, still had money out on the streets. Other inmates who knew what I did on the outside would talk to me about Billy. I'd just say, "Hey, that's his thing."

Billy had privileges. Essentially, he continued to run his business from inside the camp. Not only that, he would also organize the pools and the gambling activity at Schuylkill. We had spending accounts at the camp, but nobody carried cash. So when you placed a bet, you wagered with tuna.

You could bet a sleeve, which was three cans of tuna, or any multiple. A five- or six-sleeve bet was some high rollin'. Only thing was, you had to have the sleeves in your possession to wager them, because you were expected to pay off immediately if you lost. There was a code of honor. But they were betting a lot of sleeves, man.

A society will create its own currency, and for us, tuna was the coin of the realm. You could trade cans for all kinds of other stuff. It was the highest value item. Occasionally I would bet a little, but it just wasn't that much fun to me. I mean, the tuna was good, we ate it and it was a good thing to have around. It had protein and all of that but it was tuna, man. But they had to do something, and the tuna put value into what they were doing.

Maybe you didn't want to wager with tuna, that's okay because there was other stuff to tap into. One guy who became a friend of mine started selling stuff. He would walk around the place with a cooler that was full of alcohol. He had put it in different bottles so they didn't have the labels, but it was booze straight up. He'd say, "Man, you want to get a little taste?"

I'm like, "What?"

"Hey, you know I'll give you yours for free." For some reason he took a liking to me. Dude from Cleveland. Everybody called him Life. Not the name you'd want in prison, I would think.

I told Life, "Hell, no. I don't want any of that bootleg, no-label-havin' shit." Talk about risk versus reward: a couple of sips of liquor for a longer stretch in prison? And people did get caught. I remember one day they tested the entire camp. Everybody had to go to the administration building and blow into a Breathalyzer. There was no beating that Breathalyzer.

If I got caught doing some stupid shit like that, and my family found out about it, I wouldn't blame them if they disowned me. I could just hear them back in Detroit: "Carl. We're sending you money, driving all the way out there to see your ass, worried about you, and you're laying up in there drinking alcohol?" I did *not* want to hear that for real, so that was just not going to happen.

Remember, though, everybody in minimum security wasn't some big-time, notorious criminal. Some of them were just hustlers, like Life, so they were compelled to follow their nature and get their hustle on, even in prison. Life was like Morgan Freeman's character in *Shawshank:* He could get you almost anything you wanted. Like, if a guy wanted a pair of Timberlands, he'd have his girlfriend wear a pair into camp on visiting day, then switch them with the prison boots he was wearing. Life sold health supplements, over-the-counter stuff like Hydroxycut. He even had cell phones.

My dumb ass, I used one of his phones – once. I called Robin. I'll never forget her reaction.

"Carl. You're in prison."

"Yeah."

"And you're calling me on a cell phone?"
"Oh. Yeah."
"What the hell are you doing?"
"Getting off the phone."

I hung up in less than a minute. I saw where she was coming from immediately.

I used part of the monthly money Robin sent me to buy the maximum amount of time I could get on the prison phone, and I talked to Robin for nine minutes a day, every day, checking on her and the kids. In fact, the closest I came to having a fight while in prison was because of the phone. It meant that much to me.

Every day, at precisely the same time, I would go to the telephone. I had somebody to call, and I know that bothered some people, made them jealous, because they didn't have anyone waiting for them on the outside. But one day, this brother, Joe, tried to jump up in front of me before I got up to the phone, and it pissed me off. I was like, "Boy, why you wanna go do that?"

Nothing really happened – I managed to restrain myself – and somebody told me later that he only did it because some punks think it's funny if they can get you to do something that will make you extend your time. That's just sick, man.

One of the Mafia dudes, also named Joe, came to me later and said, "I saw what he did. Do you mind if I say something to him?" Who was I to tell him no? And do you know, Phone-Jumpin' Joe apologized to me very soon after that? Coincidence? I think not.

If my parents or anybody else wanted to talk to me, they had to go to my house and sneak in a few seconds while I was on the phone with Robin. To think I could have lost that privilege entirely by doing something as incredibly stupid as violating the rules by using a cell phone.

About a week later, I saw that her admonition was justified. One morning we were placed on emergency lockdown, which just meant we had to go back to our bunks. Then, suddenly a squad of men dressed in full camouflage gear, faces painted, came bursting into our living quarters. Apparently they had been hiding in the woods, using infrared goggles to watch prisoners who had been using cell phones in back of the building. Point taken.

I'm sure that out of that incident, Life didn't get life, but they must have come down hard on him, because I never saw Life again.

Robin and the kids came to visit me every month, like clockwork. It was a 9-hour drive each way, and the kids were little then. My mother came with them a couple of times and she was like, "You got a strong wife. This is just crazy."

Robin went so far as to put a little potty in the back of the car so she wouldn't have to stop for the children to use the bathroom. My mother-in-law lived in Pennsylvania at that time, so they would drive to her home first to break up the trip, get some sleep, and do the remaining three hours or so to Schuylkill the next morning. Because they wanted to be at my visiting hour from the beginning, which was like 8 a.m. or so, they had to get on the road at some ungodly hour, like 4 or 5 a.m. I scarcely needed reminding that what Robin was going through, what she did just to visit me, was still more proof of what an amazing woman my wife is.

Robin's visits were the highest of the highlights of my stint in prison. We quickly settled into a pattern of having a meal together being the centerpiece of our time together. Most often we would have chicken. Problem was, if you wanted the good chicken, you had to buy it when you first got there and wait until lunchtime to heat it up. If you didn't buy it right away, you could bet it would all be gone. If that happened, there were vending machines in the visiting area that sold Buffalo wings, sub sandwiches, stuff like that. Even those things would sell out fast. Man, seemed like that was some good chicken, too.

Actually, as I look back, it may be it wasn't all that good, but associated as it was with a visit from your family, that made it seem great. Keep in mind that visiting hours were the only time you could choose a pre-cooked meal: otherwise you had to take whatever the cooks dished out, or what you could concoct in the microwave. It was a novelty at first, but after six months or so I remember telling Robin, "I don't want to eat that shit anymore." It was more the ability to pick your food than the food itself that made you feel just a little like a free man.

When the weather was good for those visits, Robin and the kids and I would sit around a picnic table outside. Sometimes my little Carissa would just sit there, gazing at her daddy, or she'd just run around the table to amuse herself while Robin and I talked.

Those moments were nice, but they were painful too. All along I'd be thinking, "Man, this is a trip. They have to come all the way up here just to see me."

For sure, that Schuylkill prison camp wasn't Jackson Prison, Alcatraz or Rikers Island, but any time your freedom is restricted, your choices limited, it's punishment. If I'd had no family and no responsibilities, it would have been just a year and a half out of my life, no biggie. But being away from your family is the hardest part. Robin's father died that November, and I couldn't be there for her. Losing your father was tough enough without having your partner by your side.

My own father never came to visit me while I was in prison. And honestly, it never bothered me because I knew he had already suffered enough. Now, if my mother hadn't come, that would have shocked me to the core. Hilda would be there come hell or high water. But I wasn't surprised that Big Ed Martin didn't make it.

I'm sure he had other reasons. My guess is, given that we were busted on the same day for the same reason, he couldn't bear to see his son doing time under the circumstances. He and I didn't talk about it, then or ever.

Robin told me about one particular weekend, when they were leaving from Stratford because Hilda was coming with her. Ed was standing on the front porch, staring at the car, shifting his feet. He had the face of a kid who wanted to jump into the pool with his friends, but knew he might drown.

It was obvious: he couldn't bring himself to see me behind bars.

"It's not as bad as you imagine it to be," Robin told him. "It's not like maximum security. If you go, you might feel better about it."

"No," Ed said softly. "I can't go."

In July 2001, because I didn't drink any of Life's mystery booze, use a cell phone more than that one time, or do any other dumb shit, I was approved to serve the remainder of my sentence in a Detroit halfway house.

It was a strange transition, leaving that minimum-security prison. Hell yes, I wanted out of there, couldn't wait to get back to Detroit. But somehow it hadn't been all that bad. For sure, not anywhere near as bad as I had expected it would be before Robin and I drove up to those prison gates for the first time. I had met people who were decent to me, who taught me stuff I needed to know, who gave me insights into how a man can cope with what life deals him. There is that expression, "That which does not kill me, makes me stronger."

Well, my stretch in prison didn't kill me. I don't know how much stronger it made me, but it did give me a different perspective. It did make me appreciate all the more the things I have in life that you can't put a dollar value on. It did leave me determined to make the best life I could for my family. So I guess you could say that something useful, even valuable, came out of the time I did in prison.

I still wasn't quite home yet, though. I had been gone a full year and now I was back in Detroit, but I was kind of in transition.

My new residence was, a huge, three-story structure, on Lillibridge just off of Mack Avenue. The building is still there, although it's empty, vacant and dilapidated now. It was intended to house a large number of men as they began their transition back into society, which began with finding a job. Because I already had an occupation to go back to, someone would pick me up at the house and drive me to work in the business I already owned.

My parents came to meet with me at the real-estate office. I didn't see them for quite a while after returning to Detroit. Given how important my mother and father were to me, that may seem strange. But really, I didn't think much about it. I figured they wanted to give me some time and space to re-acclimate myself to being back. Or maybe Ed didn't know what to say to me. Whatever the reason, it was at least a few months, perhaps as late as October, before I got together with them.

We sat in Robin's office. It was the first time I had seen my father in a year and a half. At first, the conversation was light, "how are you doing?" kind of banter. Then suddenly the mood turned serious.

"We have something to tell you," Ed announced quietly.

"What is it?"

"Your mother has cancer," he said.

My mother was apologetic. "I'm sorry we didn't tell you earlier," she said, "but we didn't want to say anything while you were away and cause you more stress and worry."

They had received the diagnosis at least six months earlier. Mom was already in treatment, undergoing her first round of chemotherapy. It was a tough, heartbreaking conversation for the first day I was with both my parents again after so long.

Eventually we all hugged, they went home and I was alone in the office. I have no idea what I did there the rest of that day until it was time for me to go back to the halfway house. I do know that the same thought, or a variation on the theme, kept running through my head. "Damn! They knew about Mom's illness all this time? They had to bear that weight on their own while I was gone? C'mon! How much more can happen?"

I had barely gotten used to thinking, "Hey, I'm home for good and everything is going to be all right. Life is returning to normal and it's all going to be cool."

So much for "Happy Days are Here Again." Well, it wasn't all going to be cool. There would be new crises to overcome, pieces to pick up and put back together, a life to rebuild. Getting back to Detroit, then getting back in my own house again, these were big steps but just the beginnings of a new chapter.

The chapter that had just closed had been an ordeal, not one I was happy to go through, but not as bad as it might have been. The way I look at it, there was no choice really. The only way I could have avoided doing any time at all in prison was to give the Feds what they wanted and that was to roll on my father. No damn way I was going to do that. At the end of the day, all I have is my integrity, my honor, my family. And family has got to stick together, especially in the toughest times. That's my own personal code. That's what I live by.

Would I take the plea again, do the time? I would do it again in a heartbeat.

For now, there were new challenges to face. I had to rebuild a livelihood. I had to get back into a normal routine with my family. We still had to deal with my Dad's case and what would come of it. And biggest of all, we had to stand up to the threat of my mother's serious illness

CHAPTER SIXTEEN

Final Stat Line

It was important to my family and me that Dad be remembered as more than just a headline in a dusty old newspaper or a figure in a superficial paperback on the history of corruption in college sports.

He was much more than that, of course. But in the late 1990s, Ed Martin was known to America as "the booster who brought down the Fab Five." Some who also knew of his numbers operation surely assumed he had to be a criminal, too, a real bad guy.

My father was no saint, no Robin Hood, nor was he a one-dimensional villain in a black hat. And he was certainly much more than a footnote in sports history. His story deserved telling without the taint or stigma.

That includes one public statement that *had* to be destroyed. When Webber's back was against the wall, after he had lied to a federal grand jury and still felt the heat, he went so far as to publicly assert that Ed had preyed on the naïveté of kids. No matter how much time passes, an accusation like that cannot be allowed to linger unchallenged.

My father admired and idolized talent, loved being in its presence, no matter what form it took. He could be equally as impressed by a phenomenal chef as a champion Thoroughbred or a great athlete. He was driven to help cultivate it any way he could. If the sports world had such a designation, he would have been called a patron.

I think when he saw Joubert, Rose, and especially Webber, the kinds of players who come along just a handful of times in a generation, he was simply blown away. He couldn't help himself. Serving them in any way he could – trying to make their off-court lives easier so they could concentrate on improving their natural skills – was his way of expressing his admiration.

Ed never expected anything in return from any of the teenage athletes he sought to help except the three who asked for additional assistance and agreed to pay it back – Webber, Traylor and Taylor. There never has been any contrary evidence, even after all these years. Period.

Do I think my dad was naïve? Hell, yes, he was! He put unwavering trust in teenage boys, honestly believing they would remember his kindness, his encouragement, his financial support years after they had left his mentoring and moved on to their adult careers. Dad was thinking with his heart, not his head.

What made this all even weirder was that you'd have been hard-pressed to find a more intense, determined businessman than my father. He read. He studied. He analyzed. Like Snoop once sang, Dad had "his mind on his money and his money on his mind." He didn't go to the racetrack to bet; he went there to win. When he would forsake family get-togethers to head to the track, in his mind he was going to work to provide for his family.

He was extraordinarily disciplined. He had to be, in order to balance all his work and altruistic commitments. When he decided one day to quit his half-pack-a-day smoking habit, he just stopped. Just like that. And when it came to his numbers operation, he knew where every nickel was, who owed him and how much, what kinds of totals to expect from his runners on any given night. Why, then, did he constantly bestow such generosity and blind faith on a bunch of kids?

Two reasons, I think. One was that compulsion he had to support talent. Second, when it came to natural-born skills, Ed had them, too – not on the court or the gridiron, but in a phenomenal gift for mathematics that could not be disputed. While his skills were recognized in school, growing up with his skin color in the part of America he did, Ed never completely got over the feeling that his talents weren't cultivated to their fullest potential.

Certainly, Dad made a comfortable life for himself and his family. He traveled down many avenues to employ his math skills for financial gain, and I'm sure he made a helluva lot more money than he would have as a professor or scientist. But I think it was the not knowing, the always wondering, the "what ifs," that Dad never could completely overcome.

That's probably true for most of us. But I think you would have to be a black man in America, particularly in his era, to fully appreciate that sense of potential denied, opportunity crushed. He did not want any other young brother to feel that way, not if he could help it. So he freely opened his wallet and his heart to them, if not his common sense. He truly understood that age 14 to 18 is such a tipping point in a young urban black man's life and he desired to make sure they were guided in a positive direction.

Remember, too, that at the time, Ed didn't need the money. He was by no means rolling in it, but disposable income was not a problem. So it was easy for him to ignore Hilda's warnings and make investments in the futures of these young men. Besides, I'm sure he enjoyed being in their inner circle. It elevated him, stroked his ego a bit, and he was able and willing to pay the price for admission.

As you've read on previous pages, Ed could remember with specificity how much money he gave to which player, when the transaction occurred, and what it was for. His mind just worked that way. But he never worried about it. He didn't think he would ever really need it, but it was like a retirement account. If the three players who asked for additional assistance – Webber, Taylor and Traylor – paid back what he had extended to them after they made it big, the money would provide a nice cushion for him and Hilda entering their golden years.

With precious few exceptions, the stock he put into those ballers crashed. Ed had absolutely no way of knowing how desperate his need for money would become someday between his legal fees and Hilda's cancer treatments. And when he looked for that reservoir of goodwill he was certain would be there for him, the revenue stream was dry.

Dad died a saddened and broken man. He was carrying the stress of a federal investigation, media scrutiny, watching his beloved wife grow progressively weaker, and the absolute betrayal of people he genuinely loved, people he believed would always be there for him, all the while hearing in his head the reverberating echo of Hilda's "I told you so." When you build up that much pressure something's got to give, and I think it culminated in that embolism exploding at Henry Ford Hospital.

So what are we to make of this man? What is his legacy? What can we take away from his experiences?

As far as his numbers business in the Ford plant is concerned, the simple fact is that a Godzilla of a competitor emerged: the State of Michigan, legitimizing the previously illegal numbers business.

As for his support for high school basketball players and their families, Big Ed Martin the Super Booster may have made some bad decisions, may have trusted too much, but he did so for what he thought were the right reasons. I'm certain there are people who will always see him as a cheat and a criminal. However, it is a stark fact verified by the FBI and IRS that he never tried to influence a game, asked for a point to be shaved, or bet on the University of Michigan.

What's more, his legacy, his passion for helping young athletes, clearly left an impression on at least one of his descendants. His grandson Brandon, who furiously peddled his bicycle away from our house on the day of the raid, grew up to co-found Athlete Management Group. That's right: he's a sports agent.

"I think the exposure did help lead me in a way," says Brandon, whose current stable of clients includes four NBA and two NFL players. "It opened my eyes to different aspects of business and how to remain involved with athletes if I wasn't playing."

Brandon played basketball at University of Detroit Jesuit High School, but when his keen self-awareness told him he wouldn't be playing at the next level he began laying the groundwork for his career. "A lot of my steps toward building my practice were made at age 15 and 16," he says, "being in the mix with guys who were going to be professional athletes. Some of my best friends were among the best players in the state."

While he was a student at Eastern Michigan University, his knowledge and established relationships impressed then University of Michigan head basketball coach Tommy Amaker sufficiently to allow Brandon access to players on the team. The height of irony, huh?

"I think my grandfather, he was just going with what he knew, and what he thought was best for the kids," Brandon reflects. "It spiraled into something else, but I know his intentions were always just to help people."

His "daddy grand," as Brandon called him, would be so proud.

This is what I know about Eddie L. Martin, my dad: He was a very smart man, a passionate man, a trailblazer and an entrepreneur. He was a devoted husband, a caring father, a doting grandfather and a solid friend.

And of this I am absolutely sure: I am damn proud to be his son.

AFTERWORD

In some ways it may seem strange, but in another way, it is only fitting that a book about Ed Martin would start and end with a different person. With Hilda Martin.

In the very first pages, I dedicated this book to Hilda Martin – my mother and Ed's wife.

Now that the story has been told here, I can only end it with this question:

"Well, Mom, how did I do?"

Okay, with two more questions:

"Did I make you proud? Did we set Dad's record straight?"

I just know you're looking down from heaven and smiling. Had it not been for you, I can guarantee these pages never would have been written.

This book has been nearly a decade in the making – far longer than I ever imagined.

So many times, despite my love for my father and my desire to correct and flesh out the record, I wasn't sure it would get done. After all, Ed Martin, Mom's husband and partner all those years, is dead. He's been gone since 2003. Anyone who knew my father personally probably had an impression of the man cemented decades ago. But perhaps those memories have faded with time

But know this: I truly, deeply love my dad. And because my wife, Robin, my kids and I lived less than a mile from my parents' house, I saw him nearly every day. I didn't need a book to preserve my cherished memories.

That's not the reason I've been so obsessed with completing this.

Dad's death seemed to energize Mom even as she asked me to promise to do this. What changed her mind? What prompted such a complete turnaround? I really don't know for certain.

So if one is searching for a case history in how the actions of one person can cascade onto other lives, one need look no further than how Ed Martin's obsessive boosterism took its toll on Hilda. She had been all too prophetic when she said that if the time ever came that Ed Martin needed their help, few of the players or their families he helped would be there for him.

Without a doubt, the low point was the humiliating treatment she and Ed received from Chris Webber when they visited him at his California estate. There are wounds so deep, no passage of time can heal them, or take away the pain.

Whatever the reason, when Mom called me to her bedside for our last real conversation, she gave her blessing to the book and made me promise to complete it. "Tell the full story, good and otherwise," she said. She insisted I was the only one who truly could do it justice. I was close enough to know the inside details, she reasoned, but honest enough not to sugarcoat any of them.

I vowed that I would not let her down.

Eddie and Hilda Martin died within six months of each other in 2003. Mom told me that after he died, her husband came to her in a dream every single night until she passed away. Was he trying to apologize? To explain? To comfort? We will never know. But at least now, they're together for all eternity.

Ed Martin was by no means a saint, but he wasn't entirely a sinner, either. He was a man, like any man, with many facets, emotions, influences and motivations. And I am so thankful that his side the "Ed Martin Story" finally has been told.

You've heard the expression, a labor of love?

You're holding one in your hands.

ACKNOWLEDGMENTS

Books are seldom written in total solitude; they never come into being without the help and support of others. This book is certainly no exception. Many people helped, and in many different ways.

For me, one of the most satisfying experiences during the many years of writing this book is occurring right now: the opportunity to credit and thank those who made essential contributions. These are the people who helped me take this story from a promise responding to my mother's last wishes and to take it to reality as a book.

This was a deeply personal undertaking for me, so I ask the reader to bear with me as I personally thank those who contributed:

Robin, wife and life partner, you supported this venture from conception to completion. I hope that what we have produced here is worthy of the sacrifices that you and my family endured during its creation. As much as anyone, *The Booster* is for you. You are the person who endured these events with me. I love you and thank you for being by my side.

Mike Evans – There is no one else with whom I would have traveled this adventurous road from idea to book. This book simply would never have come to be without your boundless energy, assistance, and insistence. You knew when to lead, when to lay back and let it happen. To use a favorite Ed Martin expression: "Thanks a million!"

Marvin Evans – When you stepped in and stepped up, I knew we would do this thing. I knew that because you brought your trademark crucial calm, cadence and cognition. Those qualities are the essence of who you are, and were so important to *The Booster* project. To use another Ed Martin favorite: "Thanks ever so much."

Jim McFarlin – You got in my let's-create-a-book car along the way, but I would never have reached the destination if not for your excellent navigation. Thank you for your indispensable efforts, for helping with the words and the ways to unlock the story.

Bruce Martin – Thanks for being my big brother, for always being there when I need you.

Brandon Grier, Carissa Martin, Kelsey Martin, Kendyll Martin, Virginia and Robert Grier, Mattie Brewer and Lillian Herndon – You provided invaluable information, photographs and support for which I thank you.

Darrell Dawsey, Writer Bush, and Eric Pate, write-on brothers! My deep thanks for their insightful and candid reflections on key incidents and characters in the book, go to Tarence Wheeler, Doyle Callahan, Jimmy King, Antoine Joubert, Anderson Hunt, Johnny Johnson, Flinoia Hall, Carlton King, Derrick Maynard, Garland Mance, Edward Benavides, Anthony Jones, and Fred Hogan. Geoffrey Craig, Jonathan Troy Lewis, Pamela Freeman, Mathew Freeman, Derrick Sandifer, Dimitri Sandifer, Darryl Sandifer, Mark Talley, Dennis Archer Jr., Darryl Martin, Lanier Covington, Brian Mathis, Ossian Harris, Spencer Mott, Rochelle Moore, Monique Peek, Dwight Hunter, Ali Williams, Tamango Wallace, Dewayne Hampton, Quentin West, David and Phyllis Hill, Clayton and Rebecca Holmes, Mark Jones, Bennie Smith Jr., Jessie Keessee and Al Lucy.

Jacinta Calcut – Thanks to you and Image Graphics & Design for your outstanding efforts in design and typography of the entire book, including the artwork and execution of a dust jacket that communicates so well what the book is about.

Rebecca Powers – Your deft editorial hand elevated the text to a higher level.

Olivia Shumaker, for catching typographical mistakes that had eluded us through so many readings.

To others who helped but are not mentioned here, please forgive that oversight and know that I appreciate your contributions.

Carl Martin
April 2018